*In memory of my mother and father,
and for my children and grandchildren.*

First published in Great Britain in 1999 by Frances Lincoln Limited,
4 Torriano Mews, Torriano Avenue, London NW5 2RZ

British Library Cataloguing in Publication Data available on request

ISBN 0-7112-1315-1

Set in Bembo

Printed in Hong Kong

8 7 6 5 4 3 2 1

The God Stories

a celebration of legends

Leila Berg

FRANCES LINCOLN

AN OLD HASSIDIC STORY

The Master of the Good Name whenever a calamity threatened his people would go to a secret place in the forest. There he would light a fire. And there he would say a certain prayer to the Maker of the Universe. And the catastrophe would be averted.

When he was no longer alive, and again a calamity threatened the people, a disciple of his would go to the same place in the forest. And he would say, "Maker of the Universe, I do not know how to light the fire. But I can still find my way to the secret place. And I can still say the prayer. And that must be enough."

And it was enough. And the catastrophe was averted. Later still, calamity once more threatened the people, and another disciple went into the forest, to that secret place. And he said, "Maker of the Universe, I do not know how to light the fire. And I cannot remember the prayer. But I can still find the place. And that must be enough!"

And it was enough. And the catastrophe was averted. Years later still, when calamity once more threatened, another disciple sat sorrowfully in his chair. And he said, "Maker of the Universe, I do not know how to light the fire. I cannot say the prayer. I cannot even remember the place. All I can do is tell the story. And that must be enough."

And that was enough. And the catastrophe was averted.

CONTENTS

Author's Note

I wrote this book primarily because I wanted to give back to people the folk tales and legends which religious institutions and people in power, by dogmatism and manipulation have taken away from them.

Almost nobody reads the Old Testament voluntarily, for pleasure, today – the institutional layout, the notes, the pious paper and binding, the moralistic associations. I wanted to make a book of stories rooted in the Old Testament that would exhilarate everyone, not by taking away its poetry, a modern idea which is to me absurd, but by first taking away the religious and political and sociological manipulation; and then building not only on the stories themselves, but on the loving, fanciful improvisations that through centuries have been woven by learned and unlearned people, over them – rather like jazz.

Early in my research I came across a Staff, a Staff of sapphire, blue as the sapphire sky – a Cloak, which had pictured on it every animal, bird and insect in the world – a Book, that had in it all knowledge worthy to be told, including the song of the sun and the thoughts of the rain. In legend these gifts were given to Adam and Eve to protect them when they left the Garden of Delight, and then handed down through the ages. I decided to make them my framework, and to write the book only about the characters who in legend had been given them.

Following Jewish folklore, I made God male and female together, and the first human being male and female together, since it was made in God's image. It was also in legend made all colours, so that it could live happily and freely anywhere in the world. And the earth in legend belonged to God and was to be respected. Today we call that respect for the environment.

The God Stories is a book for people aged nine to ninety, irreligious or religious, who are captivated by stories. I hope they will read it on the train on their way to work or back, or relax with it after school; and that parents and children, grandparents and grandchildren, will read it aloud to each other for shared pleasure, as they read other books of powerful stories. It is a book for storylovers and storytellers.

God made people,
because God loves stories

THE TALMUD

The Making of the Staff

This is how it was in the beginning. There was only darkness and water everywhere. Then God decided to make the heavens and the earth. So first of all she said, "Let there be light." And light appeared.

God enjoyed the light and was pleased to have made it. He said, "I will call you Daytime." And to the dark that was still there, he said, "I will call you Night-time." Then God made the Evening to come between daytime and night-time, and the Dawn to come between night-time and daytime. And when all the four had come after each other in their right place, evening and night-time, dawn and daytime, God said, "That is the very First whole Day."

Then God looked at the water that was everywhere, and she said, "Let some of the water move upward and become the Sky." And that happened too. When she had finished making the sky, and the evening had turned to night, and the dawn to daytime again, that was the Second whole Day.

Then God said, "Let the water that is still underneath the sky flow together, so that it leaves a part where there is no water." And she said to the water that had now flowed obediently together, "I will call you Sea." And to the part where there was now no water, she said, "I will call you Earth." And he enjoyed what was done, and was pleased to have made it.

Then God said, "Let grass and all good things to eat grow out of the earth, each of them with a seed inside so that every year more will grow." And it happened just as God said. And he looked at it all and enjoyed it, and was pleased to have made it.

And evening came again and the night-time, and then came the dawn and the daytime. And the Third whole Day had come and gone.

Then God said, "Let there be special lights in the sky, a big light to rule the day and a less big light to rule the night, with the stars helping it." And they appeared in the sky as he had said, the less big light through the evening and the night-time, with the stars helping it and shouting for joy, and the big light alone through the dawn and the daytime. So the Fourth whole Day had come and gone. And God enjoyed it.

Then God said, "Let there be four-footed animals that walk on the ground, and creatures that crawl, and birds that fly in the open firmament of heaven, and great sea monsters with fins brighter than the sun, and smaller ones that swarm in the waters. And let there be many different kinds, and let each be formed in a special way, with its own shape and its own colours, and new ones growing each year in their own special pattern." And God enjoyed them all. And there was evening, and there was morning, a Fifth Day.

Then God said, "Now, not with my voice, but with my own hands, I will make a Human Being, a he and a she totally in one, just as I am totally in one."

So God took dust from the four corners of the earth, a speck from here and a speck from there. For in this way the human being would be of all colours, as the earth from different parts is of all colours, and would belong and be at peace everywhere. And she called for mist to rise from all the waters of the earth to moisten the dry dust and make it pliable. Then she took a little wind from the air, and a little warmth from all the fire, and squeezed the four together in the hollow of one hand, earth, water, air and fire. And she made a human being, copper-red and black, sweet pale olive-green and white, so splendid and shining, which, when it lay down, stretched from one end of the whole world to the other, and had heels like suns, and would live for ever. And into it she breathed the breath of life.

The breath reached its eyes, and it opened them. The breath reached its ears, and it heard music. The breath reached its feet, and it stood up.

Then said God to the angels, "Honour this human being I have made." (And ever after there were angels who were angry that they, the fiery ones, should be bidden to honour someone they saw made out of dust. And first they tried to scorch it with their flames. And when they could not, they remained alert to do the human being harm.

And others were confused at the mighty size and splendour of the creature, and ran back to God, crying, "This human being is as great as you!" And to calm them he laid a hand again on the human being, so that human size has been smaller ever since.)

Then he said to the human being that now breathed, "I have told green plants and fruit trees to spring out of the earth; and I have made seeds grow inside them so that every year fresh ones will grow, and you will never be hungry. All the four-footed animals, and the birds, and everything that creeps over the earth will eat them too, and there will be plenty for everyone. And if you are worthy, my creatures will be your delight. But if you are unworthy, my creatures will be your danger."

And God looked at everything newly-made, and

rejoiced. And as darkness began to fall, in the twilight of the evening of the Sixth Day, he made a Staff out of sapphire, blue as the sapphire sky, and signed it with her name; and the name was All-That-Is. And he put it by for a time that was not yet come.

Then God took a thin pliant branch from one of the trees and fashioned a bow, such as humans would one day use for war (though war was not yet known). And she invented seven different colours, some blazing, some tender, and painted them one by one along the curve of its length. Then he hung the bow in the sky. There it remained, invisible, till an even later time.

Then evening came and the night-time, and dawn came and the daytime, and the Sixth whole Day had gone by.

Now the Seventh Day began. But on that day, the Seventh Day, God made nothing new, except Rest and Celebration. On that day God rested. Everything stayed calmly and joyously as it was, and did not change its state, or move from one place to another, so that even the river ceased to rush by. And God enjoyed it, and celebrated it. And ever since, there are people who make nothing new on every seventh day, but joyously celebrate what already *is*, like God.

THE GARDEN OF DELIGHT

When God had made the earth and the sky and the flowing seas and all the creatures in them, he made a garden.

From all the trees she had caused to appear, she chose the ones that were loveliest, and the ones that had most luscious fruits, and the ones that gave the coolest shade from the burning sun. She put these together to make the Garden. And then, deep within them, she put two trees that were unlike any others. The mighty gold and crimson Tree of Everlasting Life, in whose shade he would rest when he walked in the Garden. And circling it round with green, weaving over it, protecting it and guarding it, the Tree of All Knowledge.

And so that everything would grow easily and generously and without too much toil, she put a river in the Garden, to flow through the earth and water it, gently and always. Then in the Garden, the Garden of Eden (which means 'delight'), she put the human being. "This garden is for you," she said. "Look after it."

Then he said to the human being, "This Garden of Delight will give you everything you need. Plants will spring from the ground. Fruits will swell on the trees. Everything will grow here for your pleasure and your nourishment, and you may eat them all. All are for you to take – except only the fruit of the Tree of All Knowledge. This you must not eat. If you do, though I made you to live for ever, you will surely die."

And she said, "I have made you last. But all that I made first, I made only for you. But do not be proud," and she laughed, for she liked the human being, "for the tiniest insect that dances in the air is older than you."

Then she called all the animals that had swiftly appeared

at the sound of a voice, both the wild ones and the gentle ones, and she called the insects, both the winged ones and the ones that crawl, and the birds that fly in the sky and the fish of the water, and they all came two by two to the human being. And each time he said to the human being, "Name this creature." And the human being spoke the name. And he said, "Yes, that is right." And that was its name for always.

Then she said to the human being, "What is your name?"

And the human being said, "It is Adam," for it was formed from 'adama', which means 'earth'.

And she laughed and said, "Yes, that is right."

Then all the creatures, with their names, went away again two by two, to their own places in the garden, to keep each other company.

Then the human creature, being alone, said, "Why have you made only one of me?"

And God said quietly, "This human being is right to complain. It is not good for a creature to be so like me – to be he and she together, so complete and so alone. I will divide this human being into two like the other creatures, a Man and a Woman, to talk with each other, to work with each other, and to keep each other company.

So God caused a deep sleep to fall on the human being; and in this deep sleep he made the division, so that from that time on the human being was a separate Man and a separate Woman, bringing together their separateness when they wanted, and keeping each other company like all other living things. And each was complete, separate and equal.

And when each saw the other half for the very first time, they held each other together as if they were still one, and kissed.

LILITH

The Woman had long hair that hung loose, and it waved like the serpentine sea. And as they lay in love together, it smelled to the Man of cinnamon. And to the Woman, the hollow under his arm smelled like apples warming in the sun. And they were as close as any two can be.

Then the Man said, "Get below me!" The Woman smiled, for she thought he was jesting. But he said again, "Get below me!"

And the Woman did not smile so much and she said, "We were made equally and together of the same dust from all the four corners of the earth."

But he said again, "Lie below me!"

And she said, "We were one body and one being, for we were made he and she together in God's own image, and we cried equally to God out of our loneliness. And that is the only reason God made us two."

But the Man said only, "Below me!"

Then the Woman said – and now she spoke more loudly and faster – "Together we named every animal that prowls the earth, every bird that wings the sky, every fish that cleaves the waters. And the angels so envied the glory and the vastness that was equally ours when we were undivided, that they cried to God, 'What is this creature that you are so mindful of it?' And yet you say to me 'Get below me!'"

And in anger she cried out the ineffable name of God. And the power of the name was so great it lifted her into the air, and she hovered above the Man. And he stood up and called, demanding, after her. Then she was gone, and he saw her no more.

And, bereft, he cried to God, "The woman you gave me has deserted me!"

So, hearing the Man, God sent three angels - Senoi, Sansenoi and Sammangelof - to find the one with the long loose hair that waved like the serpentine sea. And after many days they found her rocking on the mighty waves of the Red Sea that already murmured unceasingly of the ghosts of the Egyptians yet to come. And she now had myriads of children, fathered by the demons who lived on the seashore, and they were half-magical and grew more each day. And in anger the angels commanded her to return. But the Woman said, with scorn, "Shall I who have rocked on the waves of the murmuring sea, and heard many different voices, and had many arms round me, shall I return to the Man who says 'Get below me!' and live like a housewife?"

And the angels cried, "Do as we say!" And they cast around for a way to force her to return. And they cried, "We will kill your myriads of children!"

And the Woman of the long hair cried back, "Take care! Take care! What you do to me, I will do to others!"

"If you do," cried the angels, "we will drown you in the waters of the sea!"

"Only try!" she taunted them.

And they tried to grasp her, but over and over again she slipped mockingly through their fingers and her long hair spread through the waters like seaweed. But at last one caught her by her sun-gold arm, and another by her rosy heel, and the third by her glistening rippling hair, and they held her under the waves till she cried, "Let me go!"

But they only cried back, "Will you still kill the children of humans?"

And she struggled for air, and said, "I will spare any child who has your names above the cradle." So flattered, they released her.

But as she swam away, she cried over her shoulder, "But I will never return to the Man. I have made a bargain and I will keep to it, for I am more trustworthy than he is. But I will never return to him, for we were made equal and he would not have it so!"

And so it has been ever since. The angels killed her children daily because she remembered how she and the Man had been made all in one and equal to each other. And because they did so, she killed the children of humans (for her own are half-magical). But she kept her bargain, and spared the children who had the angels' names above the cradle – Senoi, Sansenoi and Sammangelof.

And even today there are old women who still remember. And they hang over the cradle the names of the three angels, for the whole of eight days if it is a boy child, for the whole of twenty if it is a girl; for after that time, they say Lilith has no power over them. And if a baby laughs in her sleep, they say Lilith is playing with her and beguiling her, and they wake her roughly and snatch her up. But sometimes they forget to watch, or they forget to hang up the names, or they forget the names – Senoi, Sansenoi and Sammangelof. And when they come back the child is dead, and on the coverlet a long golden hair.

THE PLOTTING OF THE ANGELS

So the Man, having lost the Woman who had been the other equal half of him, cried again to God of his loneliness.

This time, as he slept God took out a rib from him and fashioned that small part of him into a Woman. And God braided and tamed the Woman's hair, and covered her with a sheet of light smooth as a finger-nail, and adorned her with four-and-twenty rings and bracelets and necklaces. Then did God waken the Man. And the Man saw her, and kissed her. And they lived together in the Garden of Delight. And this Woman did as the Man wished.

And in that whole garden, no-one harmed another. They lived together gently and in peace, animals and insects, the birds in the air and the fish in the river, and the Man and the Woman.

And the Man remembered what God had said when the one human being was he and she together, and made out of specks of dust from here and there, in the world that held waiting the day and the night, and the sky and the sea and the earth, and the grass with seeds, and the sun, the moon and the stars, and the beasts that walked, and the creatures that crawled, and the slippery fish and the airy birds, when the human being had not yet spoken of loneliness. God had said, "I have made you last. But all that I made first, I made only for you. Yet do not be proud," and she had laughed, "for the tiniest insect that dances in the air is older than you."

And the Man told this to the Woman, and they were neither of them proud, but only delighting in their peacefulness, and in that a banquet had been laid out for them and they had been led to their place, as honoured guests.

And the Man and the Woman were naked, clothed both of them only in a sheet of light as close and as smooth as a finger-nail; and no-one was afraid.

Now some of the angels, being angry that God cared for the Man and the Woman, who had been made merely from dust when they themselves were fire, wanted to destroy them. Mightiest of them all, and their leader, was Sammael, whom some called Lucifer, Son of the Dawn, or Azazel or Satan or Iblis, for he is known in many places and by many names.

Before God had made the human being, she had said to Sammael, "You shall be the Guardian of All Nations," and had covered him with emeralds and diamonds and sapphires, with onyx and jasper and cornelian, till he was ablaze with flashing light. And Sammael was close to God, and dear.

Then God had planned to make a human being. And as he talked of this plan with the angels, asking them which of them thought well of it and who thought ill, but paying no heed to their answer – and as God, following her own wishes, gathered four pinches of dust from the corners of the earth and formed it into this creature – and when he then set it down in a Garden of Delight where there was no care and sorrow – then Sammael's anger was aflame, and he roared like a consuming fire in the wind.

"What is this creature that you are mindful of it? And why have you crowned it with glory and honour?"

"I made it," said God, and smiled. "Is it not lovely?"

"It is dust, only dust!" cried Sammael.

"You must obey it. You must honour it," said God.

"For I made it."

"No!" cried Sammael, "It is dust, and I watched you make it, and it is of no account!"

"This dust of the ground," said God, "has more wisdom and understanding than you."

"Try me," said Sammael.

So God said, "I will send all the beasts, the birds, and the reptiles before you, and if you are able to name them, this creature of mine shall honour you. But if you cannot, and if my creature names them, then shall you honour it."

So she had led the ox and the cow, the camel and the donkey before Sammael. But he knew not their names and could not speak them, and he spat with anger. Then God asked the human creature, and it spoke every name perfectly. And he had laughed, and said "That is right."

Yet Sammael had said, "Still I will not honour it!" So God had taken him and his company, all of two hundred, and hurled them out of heaven, down, down, flashing and spiralling to the earth. And there Sammael prowled, skirting the hedges of the Garden, waiting for a chance to do the creature harm.

And while he had waited, God divided the creature into two, first a Man and a Woman with long loose hair who was as proud and passionate and powerful as Sammael himself and who left the Man, and later out of the Man alone God had made a Woman with braided hair, to do as others wished her to. Then Sammael laughed, for he knew the moment had come. For this one had been made only to please the Man, and had no strength of her own.

Now there was a serpent in the Garden of Eden, a snake, who had authority. For in those days, the snake was tall as a camel, walking on legs, and with a clever mind. "Do this for me, my friend," said Sammael to him. "Turned tiny as a crumb, let me nestle in your mouth, and speak on your tongue, and I will promise you human flesh to eat which is the sweetest food in the world.

"The Man will not listen to you, for the Man is cold and churlish and hears no-one. But the Woman is warmhearted and open, and listens with gentleness to all creatures and she does as others wish her to and has no strength of her own. We will speak to the Woman, and make her anger God."

So with Sammael curled in his mouth, the snake spoke to the Woman. "There are so many trees in the Garden," he said, "all with such luscious fruit. Can you really eat all of them? Is God so good to you? Or is there just one, perhaps, you are not allowed to eat... just one?"

And the Woman said, "We can eat the fruit of every tree that is in the garden. God has given them all to us. Except, except... there is just one. The fruit of the Tree of All Knowledge we are not allowed to eat. If we eat that, God said, we will die."

And the serpent laughed. "Woman, Woman," he said, "you will not die. That is just something to say. God knows that if you eat the fruit of the Tree of All Knowledge, you will know as much as he does, that is all."

The Woman moved nearer to the tree. She thought, "It is indeed a very lovely tree, and the fruit looks very sweet, and the serpent says it will make me wise, and that I will not die... and he does seem to know... so shall I dare to try it?" And she reached out a hand and plucked a fruit from the branch and put it in her mouth.

And the Man came up to her, and she told him what the serpent had said and put the fruit to his lips, for she had been formed to think only of making him happy. And they both ate it.

It was delicious. And immediately something exciting stirred within them. New ideas rushed into their minds, and new longings into their bodies. Up till now they had done only what God had told them, but now the ideas and the longings were their own. It seemed to them there was nothing they could not do - as if everything in the world was like a fruit on a branch and they had only to put out a hand and take it.

They looked at each other eagerly. And they saw for the first time (for the light that had fitted as close to them as a finger-nail had slid away) that in the Garden of Eden they were naked. So with their new knowledge they took leaves from the tree and clothed themselves a little.

Then God's voice spoke to them as they walked through the Garden together. He called to them on the wind of the evening, as always. But this time they were afraid.

They ran and hid themselves, but the voice followed. "You have always taken delight in my company before," said God. "We have always talked together in the evenings. Why are you now hiding?"

"We were afraid," said the Man, "because we were naked."

Now God was angry, knowing all things had changed. "You have never bothered before about such things!" she said. "Who told you you were naked! Have you eaten the fruit of my forbidden tree, that everything has changed for you and you have new ideas?"

And the Man said sullenly, "I have done nothing. It was the Woman - that Woman you gave to me."

And God said to the Woman, "What have you done?"

And the Woman said, "I have done nothing. It was the serpent."

Then God said to the serpent, "I created you to be a king over all animals, cattle and beasts of the field. But you were not satisfied. I created you of upright stature and tall. But you were not satisfied. I created you to eat the same food as humankind, but you were not satisfied. I created you to speak the same language, to converse with intelligence and gaiety and subtlety. And still you were not satisfied.

"But now you shall never speak again to human beings. You shall not understand them, nor will they understand you, and you will all seek to destroy one another. You shall eat the dust of the ground, and shall no longer stand proudly upright, but slither close to the earth for ever. And you shall shed your skin again and again with a cry that will ring unanswered from one end of the earth to the other, like the cry of a cut tree, which no human hears."

Then God said to the Man and the Woman, "When the archer fires an arrow, shall he say 'It was not I, but the bow'? There is no honesty, no wholeheartedness in you.

"I see now your life will no longer be so easy and gentle. And this is no more a Garden where all live peaceably together, Man and Woman, birds and beasts, trees and flowers, as when I made it.

"For I made you to live in comradeship, without care or vexation or striving. Just by my command, I ringed you round with all things of delight, and you had no need to move your finger except to take them. So tiredness and old age would be unknown to you, and your life would be everlasting.

"But now, with your greed for All Knowledge and your lack of truth, I can see you will poison the earth that once was so sweet for you. I can see you will kill the animals that once were your friends. Your own bodies you will turn against yourselves, and tighten with pain. And you will never enjoy what you have, but only long for what you have not. And you will die from exhaustion and turn back to dust like the dust I made you from, when I had meant you to live in delight and ease for ever."

Then God made them a Cloak from the skin that the serpent shed with its silent cry, for she knew that outside the Garden of Eden they would indeed need clothing. And it shimmered, and reminded them of the far more radiant light that they had once worn in the Garden of Eden; and the smell of it, sweet and strong and dry, was of the Garden of Eden too. And some say there were embroidered on it pictures of every animal, bird and fish that God had made and the human being had named.

And they said to God, grieving, "Maker of the World, may we not take with us, into the empty world outside, spices that grow here, that we may plant and use?" And she let them gather saffron and sweet calamus and cinnamon out of the Garden, and many seeds besides, and the sprigs of fruit trees.

And as they stood up from their gathering, God gave them a Staff that was the colour of the sapphire sky, the Staff he had made on the eve of the first Sabbath; and his own name was written on it, All-That-Is.

"Lean on it," she said. Then she sent them out.

And so that they would not, when they went, snatch the fruit of the Tree of Everlasting Life too, which the Tree of Knowledge encircled, and which God no longer thought them fit for, he put there angels, who burned with twisting flame and changing shape; and they guarded the way.

So the Man and the Woman left the Garden, with their new overwhelming wonderings about Knowledge. And ever since they have tried to enter new worlds and to choose which way to follow, and the ways have got more and more in number, and more and more entangled. But the way back to the Garden of Eden stays closed.

The First Murder

Now 'Adam' had once been the name of the man-and-the-woman together, the creature formed from the dust of the earth, that is 'adama'.

Then the creature had seen how other animals were not made in the image of God, but were separately male and female, bringing their separateness together when they wanted, and talking one to the other; and it had said to God, "I am lonely. Why have you made only one of me?" So God had divided it into two separate and equal halves, and these two were called the Man and the Woman.

But the Man tried to force the Woman to be beneath him, and in anger she left him. Then God had made another Woman to do whatever the Man wished, and live only to please others, and this one stayed. And Sammael, in his jealousy, was able to destroy them, and have them sent from the Garden of Delight.

Now, after they left the Garden, the Man took again the old name Adam, but this time he took it for himself alone. And the Woman took a name that seemed new but was, secretly, very old, for it was known from the earlier time of different ways. And this name was 'Eve', which means 'Mother of All Things Living'. And some say it was one of the many names of the First One with the long unbraided hair, and that it still hung in the air like a whisper.

Outside the Garden, Adam and Eve sat down on the banks of that river that flows out of Eden, and there was no shade from the sun, and they wept.

Now it is said that there appeared before them the angel Raziel, and he held in his hands a Book. And Raziel said,

"This is a Book of Mysteries, of All Knowledge that is Worth to be Known. In it is the song of the sun, and the thoughts of the rain. In it is the echo of the speech of the thunderstorm, and the map of the four winds of the earth, and the course of the wandering moon.

"And in it are the signs that point you calamity, be it a famine, a hurricane, or wild beasts, or the fruits that drop from the tree unripe, or the death rattle that silences the city. And here too are blessings - flowers and herbs, bark of the tree and blossom on the bough - that shall solace you and heal you and be food for you. For in the world outside that is new to you there are things that are good and things that are evil, things that are important and things that are unimportant, things that are worth knowing and things that are worthless.

"And God has sent me with this Book, to read to you from it, that it shall help you find your path in the maze, lest you be blinded by the abundance of so many ways."

And they ceased their weeping, and raised their heads and listened, as he read to them from the Book.

And he read to them of fire-tongs, of the hammer of the smith, and of the oxen that pull the plough, and many things like these that were not yet on earth but were still to come. And he told them how to call up angels to reveal things or to change them.

And what he read was so amazing that at times they marvelled, and grew cold, and once they fell down affrighted, so close was it to sorcery. But he said to them, "Be not afraid. Be of good courage, and learn, and teach others. For this is the Book from which all things worth knowing can be understood."

And he left the Book with them and they studied it. And it was in this Book that Adam read of King David who had not yet been born, and he said to God "Who is that man?"

And God said, "He is a bold man, and a singing man, and a fighting man, and a loving man. And the people cheer him."

And Adam said, "How many years have you given him, God?"

And God said, "Thirty years."

And Adam said, "And how many years have you given me?"

And God said, "One thousand."

Then Adam said, "God of the Universe, be not angry at my ungraciousness, but give David seventy of mine."

And it was so agreed, and David the king and the lover was later born, and lived a hundred years instead of the thirty that God had given him, because Adam had seen the Book.

And it was with this Book, together with the directions of God, that Noah years later built the ark, and sheltered the animals, and grew healing herbs in the new world.

And with it, King Solomon who had a thousand wives built a house of crystal glass to receive the Queen of Sheba, and with it he sought out a worm who could split rocks so that he might build his Temple. And with it he understood the language of all creation, the trees and the flowers of the earth as well as the beasts and the birds, and heard the lilies murmur one to another as he passed by, "What nonsense these humans talk. We are more beautiful than he." And heard the nightingale say to her beloved, "That one has a thousand wives, but none love him as I love you." And he bowed his head. But these stories are still to come.

Now in the world outside the garden, Adam and Eve had the first two children. They called them Cain, which means 'I know I can keep what I want', and Abel, which means 'I know everything passes and cannot be held'. And Adam thought he would one day give the sapphire Staff that bore God's name, and the shimmering Cloak and the Book of Knowledge, to one of them.

Adam and Eve said the whole world was for their children. So Cain said "We will divide it."

"I will take what stands still, for that I can hold," said Cain.

"I will follow what moves and changes," said Abel.

So Cain dug the land. And although it was now hard to dig, and nothing would grow without work, yet the fruit of it still tasted of Eden. And Abel tended the sheep and the lambs, who came to him and skipped away, as they had done with the Man and the Woman in Eden, and he wandered with them over hills and streams.

But as time went by, Cain said more and more in his heart, "This is mine, I can hold it," as if the earth belonged to him, and not to God. And God was angry with him, for God had put human beings on earth only to look after it for a while, for the earth was God's.

Now it came to pass that it was the time of offering gifts to God. Abel offered a lamb, while Cain offered fruits from the trees, and vegetables from the ground. But Cain chose ones that were bruised by falling, or cut by the spade, for he said to himself, "They are mine," and he grudged giving them. And because of this, and because Cain laid plans and forced the earth to give what he wanted (so that God said, "That is for honouring Cain, not for honouring me; for my honour is what bursts forth of its own energy and joyousness"), because of these two things God would not take his offering, only Abel's. So in his heart Cain hated Abel.

Now it happened that Abel was leading his sheep one day to pasture. Cain barred his way saying, "This land is mine. Go elsewhere with your sheep."

And Abel answered him, in surprise, "If the land is yours, and the sheep are mine, then why do you take their wool for your clothing? If you will pay for the wool from the sheep that are mine, then will the sheep and I fly through the air, without touching the land that is yours!" And he laughed.

And Cain raised his spade and struck him down. And Abel's blood ran along the ground, and he died.

Then God said to Cain, "Where is Abel, your brother?"

And Cain shrugged, and said, "I know not."

And God said again, "Where is he?"

And Cain said, in anger, "Am *I* my brother's keeper?"

And God said, "What have you done! The voice of his blood cries to me from the ground where it runs. And the ground, blood-soaked, shall ever remember. It shall grudge you your food from this day forth. And a fugitive and a wanderer shall you be on earth for ever."

Then Cain cried, "Is my sin too great to be forgiven? What shall become of me? If you drive me away, and hide from me your face, and the earth, obeying you, will not feed me - if a wanderer and a fugitive I shall be for ever - then how can I live? For whoever finds me weak and unsheltered will kill me!"

And God said, "No, that is not my way. I will keep you safe. And she set a mark on Cain's forehead saying, "This is the mark of pardon. By this mark, all shall know you. And they shall not dare to harm you, for Abel's sake. But it is not the mark of forgetting, but rather of remembering."

And some say too that she gave Cain a dog to walk by his side in his wanderings, and drive off wild beasts and violent men who might be a danger to him. For there are many stories. God did indeed keep him safe, but sent him out of that land for ever, to be a fugitive, solitary and wandering to and fro, in that country of exiles that all call Nod.

And afterwards, when God allowed him to rest, Cain, the man who had murdered his brother, became the very first human being to build a city, and to wall it round, and force people to stay in its boundaries. And he was the very first to make tools for weighing and measuring and counting. And to the city he had built he enticed travellers, and tricked them and robbed them, that he might have more to weigh and count. But that was yet to come.

In the meantime, the rift between earth and humankind grew greater still. And indeed, ever after, though Cain believed the earth was his, he could dig from it not fruit that still tasted of Eden but only thorns and thistles; and the vine, that even outside Eden had grown a thousand kinds of grape, now grew only one.

But within the field where he had died, the body of Abel lay on the ground, and Adam and Eve wept for him. Slavering beasts crept close, and birds flapped screaming round him; and Abel's sheep-dog drove them away, guarding his master. No-one had ever died before, and no-one had been buried, and they did not know what was to be done, bar grieving.

But one day, a raven scratched away the earth with his beak, to make a hole for his dead nestling, and they saw what he did. So they learned from the birds, and buried Abel. That was the very first death, and the first burial.

The Flooding of the World

So it came about that neither to Cain nor to Abel did Adam and Eve give the Sword and the Cloak and the Book that had come from the days of Eden. For both these sons were lost to them in one bitter day. And they grieved for them many years.

But when at last they ceased their sorrowing, another son was born to Eve. And this one they called 'Seth', for that means 'consolation'. And to him they gave the three wondrous things.

And with the Cloak and the Staff and the Book of All Knowledge that is Worth Knowing, Seth became a wise man of the sky, an astronomer, knowing the course of the planets and the breath of the four winds and the paths of the sun and moon; and many came to him, to ask of their present and of their future.

It came to pass that one day Seth read in the Book that the world would be twice destroyed, once by fire, once by water. And he was filled with sorrow for the people that were to come.

And straightway he called to his wife and children, and all building together they fashioned two mighty pillars, one of brick and one of stone, so that one pillar at least might survive the holocaust.

And together, on each pillar, they wrote the mysteries and revelations and prophecies of the Book, according to the space thereon. And at the bottom of each pillar they wrote, "There is another column. Seek that and read likewise." For they wished that whoever survived the end of the world would have All Knowledge that is Worth

Knowing to guide them in their loneliness.

And it is said that these pillars stand, to this very day, because of Seth, in a land called Seiris or Syriad, and travellers have seen them; but where this land is, none now remember.

And when Seth in his time had died, and also his wife and children, the Book and the Cloak and the Sword passed from hand to hand, from child full-grown to child new-born. And at last they came into the hands of a child whose name was Methuselah.

And it is said and sung that when Methuselah was grown, he took the Staff which was also a Sword, and slew many thousands of demons. Ninety-four times ten thousand did Methuselah slay. And some say, not once only, but every single minute. But that is another story.

Now when Methuselah was bent with many years, that was the time when giants walked the land, and the earth trembled. And this is how it came about.

When God had made the human being, the man-and-woman-in-one who named itself Adam, God had hurled two hundred angels out of the sky; for these were jealous ones who would not honour Adam; and they streaked to earth like shooting stars. And while the human being became a separate Man and a separate Woman, first a woman with long golden hair, passionate and proud, and the equal of the man, then a woman who did only what the man wished, and when Sammael, lurking at the gate of Eden, plotted to destroy them, and they ate of the forbidden tree and were driven from the Garden of Delight, and their children became a murderer and one who was murdered, all this time these angels walked unseen among humans.

And now they saw the daughters of Cain. And the daughters of Cain were beautiful.

So it was, that wishing to be close to them, the angels took on the shape of humans themselves. They spoke to the daughters of Cain, and they smiled with them, and they taught them things they had not known before. How to make bracelets and ornaments, how to make paint to beautify the eyelids, and to make scarlet the soles of their feet. How to perform sorceries of all kinds. How to make musical instruments that entrance the heart, and how to sing in cheerful voices. How to make mirrors in which one can see not only oneself, but even what lies behind one. And how to make swords and spears with which to murder. All this is told in song and story.

And now the fallen angels made union with the daughters of Cain, and they had children. And the giants who walked the earth in those days, the mighty ones of terror that were sung of old, were their children; and they brought desolation to the world.

Very huge and terrifying were they. Their own mothers, the daughters of Cain, were as fragile grasshoppers before them. They devoured all that humankind produced, and still they were ravenous. Then they began to devour humankind itself. And humankind, which had once had one language with the beasts and the birds and the fish of the sea, and had lived in sweet companionship, began to devour them all, beasts and birds, fishes and reptiles, and all the creeping things that scuttle over the earth; and they drank their blood. And the earth was cold with dread.

Then the beasts remembered what God had said to the human being who was made in God's own image, he and she in one, when the world was six days old. He had said, "If you are worthy, the beasts shall be your delight. If you are unworthy, they shall be your danger." So in that time of terror, when the humans were unworthy, the beasts no longer had love for them, nor loyalty, nor fear, and they turned on the humans and killed them, lest they be killed themselves.

And the whole earth was as ravished as a field when locusts have passed, and it cried out to God. And God said, "I will destroy them all, and make a new world."

So it was that God turned to Methuselah, for Methuselah and his grandson Noah alone were honourable and wholehearted.

And by then Methuselah was ancient in years, walking slowly with a Staff that was older than Methuselah himself, and sapphire as the sky; and some say he was a king. And God said to Methuselah and Noah, "You will I save. Therefore build you an ark out of gopher wood, for gopher wood rides lightly on water. Three storeys build it, with a window, and with a door to one side; and make rooms therein. And you must spread pitch both within and without, to withstand the water.

"For once your ark is ready, the East wind will blow. And I shall bring upon earth, and upon all living things within the earth, a flood that is overwhelming. And all that are not in the ark will perish, and their deeds with them!"

Then he told them, number by number, the measurements each part of the ark should be, for he was a Maker as well as one who made things appear, and had squeezed together and moulded the first human being.

And she said to them, "Take up the Book of All Knowledge that is Worth the Knowing. For in that Book can be read the secret of gopher wood, and how one may hide from a torrent of water and live. And in it also are all the secrets of healing, by trees and flowers and roots and seeds." So they took it, and read, and gathered in the gopher wood for their lives' sake.

Then began they to build. They worked slowly, for they were full of grief, and they wished the people and the beasts to have time to change their ways, for then, they thought, God's plans might also change.

But even as they continued to work the giants mocked them, saying they themselves could hold their heads high above any floodwater, and should God open the sluices of the deep, they would block the cavity with their feet. And men and women came, laughing, to ask why were they building a boat so far from the sea. "What is this deluge?" they cried. "If it be water that breaks from the earth, we will bring sheets of iron and pave the land, to hold it down. If it be water that pours from the sky, we will bring awnings to make roofs over our heads!"

And the beasts themselves came and went as they willed, in among their work, and defiled it wantonly and scornfully.

So Noah and Methuselah continued to build, and they became silent.

The building being so long-drawn-out, and Methuselah being already most marvellously old, he knew he would surely die before it was finished. So he gave to Noah his Staff, his Cloak, and the Book of Mysteries in its golden casket. For they had come to him from his father, who years before had had them from his own father. And long before that, they had come from Seth, the third child of Adam and Eve.

And when Noah took them, that very same day Methuselah died, being nine hundred and sixty-nine years old. And Noah wept for him.

And so amid his weeping, Noah continued to build alone.

When the Ark was ready, and sealed with pitch within and without, Noah took the Sword of Methuselah that once was Adam's, and placed it safely inside. And he took the Book of Mysteries which they had studied together, and he put that inside also; and with it the glimmering Cloak of snakeskin that had been brought out of Eden to cover the coldness of the Man and Woman, and to protect them. And the Three Gifts lay together in a corner of the Ark.

Then God said to him, "In seven more days I will cause it to rain, and it shall not cease for forty days and forty nights. And for a whole year will the waters lie upon the earth.

"This shall you do. Of every living creature both of the land and of the deep, and such as hover aloft or wing the air, you shall bring two into the Ark with you, male and female, to keep them alive. And you shall also take enough of all food that is eaten, and it shall be food for them and food for you."

Whereupon Noah's heart, already heavy, was smitten like withered grass. And he cried out, "Maker of the World, have mercy!"

For on the day Adam and Eve left Eden, was closed the mouth of all beasts, so that they could no longer speak out words, and was closed the ears of humankind so that they could not hear; though till then all had spoken one with another, with one lip and one tongue.

"How shall I fetch them, God?" cried Noah. "For we

cannot speak or explain one to another. Nor have I ever been a hunter. And I have not the strength – for I am now alone – to collect all the animals into the Ark!"

And God heard him. So he spoke to the angels. And they came down, bringing baskets of food of myriad kinds, so that the animals, smelling and savouring it, gathered of their own accord and followed the angels and Noah need not either call them or drive them.

In the same way as they had come before the first human being for naming, so did they come before Noah. The ox, and the cow, and the camel and the donkey. The leopard and the lion, and the graceful giraffe who has eyelashes like little waterfalls. And the storks, whom people had called the Loving Ones, for they cared so tenderly for their young. And the dolphins who are half-fish and half-human, and love humankind. And the whales singing their sea-song. And the wild ass that sniffs the wind, and the horse that paws the ground. And the clever fox. And the ostrich that has little wisdom, and the tiny ant who has much. And the tamed ass that is much enduring, and came at his own slow pace, saying to himself, "It is only because I am wanted to carry wood or water. Yet will I come."

And the little lizard who slips in a crack like the flick of an eyelid, and the huge one who tramples the undergrowth like an army. And Ziz, who is king of the birds, and Behemot, hippopotamus-like, who is king of the beasts and who, it is said, grazes on a thousand mountains in one day, and since he is mild as he is large shelters the lesser beasts from the sun with his bushy tail, and the birds also with his tail held higher. And there were many more.

Of unicorns, since a unicorn only one day old is as big

as a mountain, Noah could take only one. And round this one's horn, he put a rope, fastening it to the Ark, so that the unicorn might follow safely behind. And some say that Og, king of the mocking giants, cunningly leapt on his back, and so escaped also; and that Noah made a hole in the wall of the Ark and fed the two of them. (And for this, Og, king of giants, grovelled, and swore to be forever the slave of humans; but he lied and became their enemy. But that is a separate story.)

So it was that save for the one unicorn, and the one giant, all living creatures came two by two into the Ark. And they took their places, the birds on the top storey, the beasts and crawling things on the bottom storey, Noah and his family in the centre. And God shut them in.

And it came to pass in seven days' time, on the seventh day of the second month, the East wind blew. And God took two stars from the Pleiades; and the waters of heaven rushed downwards through the holes. Then he pulled back the bolt that held fast the double doors of the deep, and the great seas exploded upwards.

So the waters from below and the waters from above were joined together, as they had been at the very beginning before the world was made. And they boiled and steamed for forty days and forty nights, buffeting and tossing the Ark so that all inside were hurled to and fro like beans in a seething pot.

And every single creature in the Ark, according to its nature, uttered aloud its own particular cry of fear, of sorrow, of rage or desolation. And the sound of all cries together was like the earth rending itself apart.

The wild ass that is used to the wilderness howled at

his restraint. The swift unrelenting camel screamed piteously to traverse again her ways.

The lions in their anger would have leapt on all living, and emptied the Ark. But they were sick and dazed from the turbulent seas, and lay still, only snarling. Even so, one attacked Noah, so that ever after he walked crookedly. But in time their sickness grew so great that they wanted nothing, and Noah was freed from delicately fetching food for them.

Some ate by day, and some by night, as had been their custom. Some ate at the first hour, some at the sixth or the eighth. So Noah had no rest from moving to and fro. Moreover, Noah was sore put to fill their need, and to find the right food to sustain them. For the camels ate straw, the asses rye, and the elephants the little shoots of vines. And what was food meet for chameleons Noah knew not. He gave them pomegranates and they spurned them. But when they were near to death from starving, it happened that a worm fell from the rotting fruit, and they liked it well. So the many apples that rotted on the Ark, those Noah gave them, and they were satisfied.

In that whole year of darkness and howling, only the phoenix who has the feet and tail of a lion, and the head of a crocodile, and twelve wings like an angel, made no demand, and, when sought out to be given food, said courteously, "I see you are hard-pressed; I will disturb you not." And this Noah heard, and was astonished, for it was long since animals or birds had spoken to man, in anger or in peace.

And for this, it is said in song and story that the phoenix lives for ever. And it rides with the galloping sun, both of them singing together. (For it is known it is the sun's song that keeps it moving, and to make it stand still one must only order "Be silent!")

So in the tumult of the Ark, when only the phoenix had care for him, Noah raised his voice in despair and cried aloud, "O Maker of the Universe, release me from this prison! My soul is wearied by the stench of lions, bears, and panthers!"

Then did God say to Noah, "Have you not the Book, that I gave long ago to Adam and Eve? Read it and you will understand the mysteries that unfold around you."

And Noah said, "God, it is dark in this Ark. How shall I see to read pages?"

And God said, "Look about you. Do I not provide?" And Noah looked, and he saw that light glowed from the corner of the Ark where lay the sapphire Staff, the Book in the golden casket, and the shimmering Cloak.

"I will read when I can, God," he said mildly, "but you know, God, I have little time for reading."

So for a whole year, the waters prevailed upon the earth. And at first Noah could not distinguish night nor day one from the other, for there was no light from the sky in all that time. But the light that shone from the corner was more brilliant at some times than at others, and he saw that those times were nights. Yet still he knew not either cold nor heat, day nor night, summer nor winter, seed-time nor harvest.

And upon the earth all died that moved, birds of the air, and wild beasts, and beasts of the field, and every creeping thing, and all human beings, and all giants. But Noah remained alive, and they that were with him in the

Ark, and the two that were roped behind. For the waters upheld the Ark, high and safe, and the Three Gifts gave a soft blue light in the worst of darkness, so that all could be fed.

Then at the end of a year God remembered Noah and the Ark. And she made a wind to pass over the earth, a breath of life. It drove the waters of the deep toppling over the earth's brink. The fountains of the sea ceased their leaping, and the windows of heaven closed, and God plugged the Pleiades tight again with two stars that she took from the Great Bear. (And ever since the Great Bear pursues the Pleiades, growling night after night, "Give me back my stars!")

Then slowly the waters retreated. Slowly the Ark came down. On the seventeenth day of the seventh month, it came to rest on the mountain of Ararat, which was still covered with water. And still the waters retreated. Till in three more months the highest part of the mountain showed, with the Ark resting thereon.

And in forty more days, Noah opened wide the window. "Go forth," he said to the raven, "and bring news of the world outside." But the raven hid under the wings of the eagle, and feigned not to hear him calling.

Noah was angry, and took hold of it, and cast it out. But it only flew to and fro in his sight, and returned. He cast it out again, and again it straightway returned. Once more he cast it out and this time it came not back. But Noah knew it was feeding on drowned men floating in the waters, not that the land was dry.

Then he said to the dove, "Go thou forth then." And she flew sweetly out. But she could find no resting-place for the sole of her foot, and she too returned unto him, to the Ark. And Noah put out his hand, and took her in again.

Seven days more he waited. Then again he sent out the dove. This time, she stayed away till the evening. And when she returned, in the eventide, in her mouth was an olive leaf, freshly plucked. So did he know that the tips of the trees were now showing.

Seven days again Noah waited, then sent forth the dove once more. This time returned she not, but stayed in the world outside, where the trees stood free of the water and held out their arms for nests. And she waited for her mate.

So it came to pass, on the first day of the first month, that Noah took off the canvas of the Ark, and climbed through the skylight, and looked out. The surface of the land was clear to see, a stretch of gleaming silver.

And as day followed day, and the silver mud grew more and more dry, and the time for leaving the Ark drew nigh, Noah remembered Methuselah's Staff and the Book in the golden casket and the glimmering Cloak, and he went to fetch them.

But only the Staff and the Book were there. The Cloak had gone. He sought for it throughout the Ark, even to the upmost deck where the birds had huddled, and the lowest deck that had been full of the stench of beasts large and small, and tiny creeping creatures. But he found it not; and he mourned for it, for it had come to him from his friend Methuselah, and before that from fathers and grandfathers now dead.

On that same day the whole land was dry. And God said to Noah, "Go forth." And the dainty gazelle leapt free and paused on the threshold. And all of Noah's family, and all the birds of the air, and beasts, and everything that creeps on the ground, and all living things that were in the Ark, silently surveyed the empty earth.

Then God said, "Now may ye live and multiply, and fill the earth, and celebrate life. The beasts of the field grazing new grass, the birds hovering aloft on clean winds or winging the pure air, and the wild beasts roaming again after dark, and returning to their lairs when the sun rises, as wild beasts did before." And all the people and the animals and all creeping things and the birds followed each other out of the Ark. And the dove in the olive tree called to her mate.

But Noah hesitated. For he thought in his heart, "Why should we wish to people the earth, if God will again destroy us?"

And God caught his thought, and said, "This do I promise. Never again will I send a flood to destroy all that lives." Still Noah did not put foot on the ground, for it seemed to him that life was made out of danger and sorrow and toil, and all was vanity.

But God said, "Be not afraid. As long now as the earth remains, there will always be heat and cold, day and night, summer and winter, seed-time and harvest, to follow each other in the sweet certain order you knew before I unplugged the stars." But still Noah hesitated.

Then God said, "Noah, hear me. I will set a seal on my promise. Long ago I hung a bow in the sky, and it was invisible; for I waited this time's coming. But from now, whenever the sun trembles at the power of the rain, and human beings grow afraid, my rainbow shall glow out of the sky to be a sign of that promise."

And immediately the rainbow shone out from the sky,

and the seven colours painted along its curve were tender and strong. And at last Noah put away doubts and stepped down from the Ark.

And he carried with him the Book in its golden casket, and the sapphire Sword. And it is said that with the aid of the Book, he made, in the empty and clean-washed world, plants to grow that would heal humankind. And so that men and women would no longer have to work with their bare hands only - as they had had to do after leaving the Garden of Delight - he made the very first plough, and the first sickle, and other tools beside. And from the grapes he made the very first wine, that rejoicing might come of labour, and balance it (though there are some who have reproached him for this).

All this he learned from the Book of Mysteries and Knowledge that is Worthy to be Known, and gave it to humankind. And some say that is why he had been given the name of Noah, for 'noah' means 'rest' and 'comfort'.

But all this was to come later. And in the meantime, the glimmering Cloak was lost.

THE HIGH TOWER OF BABYLON

Once there was only one language. People and animals, birds and fishes, the insects that fly and the insects that crawl, all spoke to one another. Each spoke, and each listened to the speaking, and answered; and they were companions.

But when Adam and Eve had listened to the voice of the serpent, whom the jealous angels had told to destroy them, and wanted All Knowledge for themselves, then God had said, "You are no longer part of the family-of-the-world that I have made, that was to hold together everything living. Now there is a line between you and all other living things. And on each side of the line you will be enemies, with different languages."

Then came the time of the fallen angels, and the giants, their children, who laid waste the earth; and humans became wicked and unworthy. And remembering what was said in the beginning - for God had said to the man-and-woman-in-one, "If you are worthy, the beasts will be your delight. If you are unworthy, they will be your danger" - the animals fought the humans. So the humans began to hunt them, killing and using them, though once they had lived gently together, eating the same food, sweet easy food of the earth, and playing together (and some say that time will come again, but that is another story).

So, bit by bit and more and more, human beings ceased to understand other living things. Eventually they understood only other human beings, who were still together of one language and one speech. But in the time of the building of the high tower, that too changed, so that human beings did not even understand each other. And this is how it came about.

Now it is said in song and story that when the Ark rested on Ararat, and all the earth was silver-wet, and the beasts, the birds, the creeping things, and all men and women who had escaped therein were crowded on the threshold, the youngest son of Noah stole the Cloak, the glimmering Cloak of snakeskin. For he was less than a hundred years old and still behaved childishly.

(For when God made the first human being, man-and-woman-in-one, he meant it to live for ever. And only when Adam and Eve stole a taste of the fruit of the Tree of All Knowledge, did God make them mortal. So it was that Adam, instead of living for ever, lived only nine hundred and thirty years. And as time went by, moving ever onwards from the Garden of Delight, human life became shorter and shorter, till in our time few live to be a hundred. But in the time of Noah's youngest son, to be one hundred years old was to be just coming out of childhood.)

So it was that Noah, the glimmering Cloak having been stolen from the Ark, took with him on to dry land only the sapphire Staff and the Book of All Knowledge Worth Knowing. And he gave them to his middle son Shem, whom he loved; for Shem's life and wholeheartedness were as his own. And together they read of the laughing stars, and the wandering moon, and they learned all the voices of the winds.

Now the youngest son of Noah who had stolen the Cloak hid it for many years. And all that time none knew where it was. But when he was a grown man he took it from its hiding-place, and secretly gave it to his son; and one day his son gave it to the child of his old age who was sweet to him, whose name was Nimrod.

And when Nimrod reached the age of twenty years, he put on the shimmering Cloak of snakeskin which had been long hidden. And he was wise and mighty; and it seemed at first he was wholehearted, for with the Cloak he heard the thoughts of animals, and he understood the secrets of their heart. But it was only that he might slay them.

He was never lacking in meat to eat, or skins to clothe himself. No wild animal could hide from him nor hurt him. And men and women fell down at his feet and begged him to spare them alive, because in the lust of his power he killed all living things.

And it is said that he built for his own glory a fortress on a round rock. And above that he built a throne of cedar-wood, and above that a throne of iron, and above that a throne of copper, and above that a throne of silver, and above that a throne of gold. And at the topmost top, he set a huge blazing jewel. And there he sat, astride his jewel. And all worshipped him, and called him Nimrod Amraphel. And he became one of the ten mightiest Kings of the whole earth.

Now at this time, to one of his commanders was born a son, whose name was Abram. And it is said in song and story that on the night this child was born, a comet came from the east, and streaking across the sky swallowed four bright stars that were each in a different quarter of heaven. And when his courtiers spoke of this, Nimrod did cry out with a long loud cry. For he had the Cloak of Adam and Eve, and was versed in signs and wonders. "That comet is a mighty child who will conquer me and bring me down. Seek out the child that was born tonight, and kill him!"

So the officers and soldiers and slaves of Nimrod sought to do as he commanded. And because hundreds of children were born that night, they killed them all. And they thought they must surely have killed the dangerous one.

But the mother of Abram had wrapped up the child, and taken him to a cave whereof she knew, by the River Euphrates, and there she had hidden him. And in ten days only, he stood up and walked. And in ten days more, he was a full-grown man. And this man left the cave, and he sought out Shem and Noah, who still lived though wondrous old, and he studied the Book of Mysteries with them that he might know the ways of the Maker of the World, and he learned the dance of numbers, and how to call down angels, and how to banish demons, and all Knowledge Worth Knowing.

Now during this time, the captains and guards and soldiers of Nimrod had talked together, and they said, "Let us build a new city to add to the glory of Nimrod. And in the middle of it let us put a tower for Nimrod, so high that the top of the tower shall reach into heaven. No floodwaters will ever reach him, and no enemies ever harm him. Inside his tower he will be impregnable; and we shall be mighty with him, and he will care for us."

So they journeyed east, to find a flat place to build. And when they had settled on a place, they began to make bricks (for there were no stones in that ground), and they used clay to hold the bricks together, and dried the bricks in the sun, then in the fire to make them stronger. And they began to build. The tower, which they continued to build, they called Babel, and they called the city Babylon.

And while they continued to build the tower, they grew

excited, and beyond reason, and they began to speak wildly. "What right has God to take all the upper part of the world, leaving us only the lower?" one cried. And another said, "Let us climb into heaven, and take it!", and another said, "Yes, and with swords and spears and arrows we will capture God! And we will avenge ourselves for the drowning of our forefathers!"

They built the tower seven miles high. Seven stairways made they in the eastern side by which they climbed to the top, and seven stairways on the western side for descending. And it took a man one year to hoist a brick to the top. So was it that when a brick fell to the ground again, they were filled with despair, and wept, and tore their hair; but if a man fell, they paid no heed, and they did not pause.

Even a woman giving birth was not allowed to leave the tower. For the building of the tower had become more important to them than life itself. And still they continued to speak in this wild way.

Now it happened that Abram wandered one day to the plain where men and women were building the tower for the glory of Nimrod. And now the tower stretched up seven miles towards heaven. And Abram watched. And he saw that if a brick fell from the top, the builders were in despair; but if a man or woman fell they cared not. And he marvelled, and returned home, and told it to Shem.

And on that same day, because they were both amazed and angry at the tower and at the doings of men and women, Shem gave Abram the Staff of Adam, the Staff that was blue as the sapphire sky, which God had given to Adam and Eve when she sent them out of the Garden of Delight. And Shem told Abram how with the Staff Methuselah had slain millions of demons, and how it already vibrated with the crashing of the Red Sea which one day it would command to part its waters, but that day was yet to come. And Abram took the Staff for his own.

But on the high tower on the plain, the people of Nimrod began to storm heaven. And they began to shoot arrows into the sky. And God's angels caught every one, and to deceive them sent each back, dripping blood, so that the archers cried with glee, "Now we have killed all heaven's minions!" And they built more greedily than ever, now meaning to seize the empty heaven.

God watched them. And she came down to see the city and the tower, which the children of men were building. And he said silently, "Behold, they are one people and they have the same one language. And this is what they begin to do."

And God watched a little longer, and again spoke, this time out loud. "Nothing is enough for you. When you are united, you are strong. But in your strength you are greedy beyond belief. I will tell you: from this day forth you will not understand even each other. And this great family-of-the-world that I made, which was to hold together everything living, will be broken into little fragments, each at war with everyone else; and it will not even hold together everything human."

And as God spoke, an East wind blew through the Tower of Babel. And the speech of all of them broke up into different languages, and no-one could understand anyone else.

They were astonished at one another. They asked for things, and the things were not given. They gave things that had not been asked for. Questions were not answered, and they mocked one another. So in their anger they left off building the tower, they hurled mortar and bricks at one another, and then drew their swords.

On that day, because of the Tower of Babel, half the human race was destroyed. And the rest that still lived, God took and scattered over the whole face of the earth, east and west and north and south, with their different languages and with their lack of understanding for each other. And that is how it is now.

As for the Tower itself, earth swallowed a third, fire from heaven another third. Yet the third that remains to this day is still so tall that from its summit, the distant groves of Jericho appear as swarms of locusts, and the high air robs men of their wits. And it is said that if anyone only passes by, the thin finger of confusion reaches out from the broken tower and touches him delicately, and he forgets all he has ever known.

THE PRINCESS IN THE CHEST

When Nimrod found the child of the dream had escaped him, he sought furiously to capture him. And many are the songs and stories of their meetings. It is said that once he threw him into a furnace. But the flames crouched down into flickering candle-lights and died away, and the wood burst into blossom and then into fruit. And the furnace became a pleasure garden where Abram walked at ease, and smiled to Nimrod. And Nimrod was most dread afraid. That was the time when Nimrod in fear heaped gold and silver and crystal treasures on Abram, and gave to him, unasked, his chief slave Eliezer, who was tall as a cedar tree, with a stride of three whole miles, and a mighty warrior, so that he be not at war with him.

So Abram grew unhurt to manhood. And he married. And his wife Sarai, which means 'My Princess', was one of the four most beautiful women in the world. Flushed as a pomegranate were her cheeks, and her long black hair fell in ripples like an eagle's wing. Only Abigail, Esther, and Rahab were to be her equals, and each would be as different as a lily from a rose; but they were not yet born.

Now it is said in song and story that God spoke to Abram, saying, "Leave your country, and your kindred, and your father's house, and I will show you a land flowing with milk and honey; and it shall be yours. And I will make of you a great nation, as many as the grains of dust on the earth or the countless stars in the sky."

So that Abram and Sarai, and Lot his brother's son whom he loved, took all that they had, and went out of the land where they lived.

And when they came to the borders of Egypt, Sarai knelt to bathe her face in the river that travellers call 'The Torrents of Egypt'. And so lovely a face did Abram see reflected in the water, that he was afraid, and said, "When the Egyptians see you, they will kill me. But you they will take and keep alive. Say therefore that you are only my sister, that it might be well with me - and let them do with you what they will." (For this was a long time since the days of Lilith, who was proud and equal with the man. And now since Eve a woman did only what a man wished.)

So Abram shut her up in a chest, in all her finery, and had her carried over the border for his own safety's sake.

But an officer of Pharaoh, the great King of Egypt, seeing that the chest was large and heavy and that Abram was mindful of it, enquired of Abram of its contents. And since Abram answered him in a wandering way, as one uncertain of the best answers, the officer opened the chest. And he saw Sarai. And all the people were instantly still, and marvelled, for she was the fairest woman neath the sky.

Then, exultant at her beauty, a prince of Pharaoh's household broke into song, carolling like a bird, pouring out golden words like wine brimming over a goblet, weaving phrases about her like sweet garlands. And ever after, minstrels in their songs have praised her radiant eyes, and her delicate hands, and her gleaming hair, for the prince's song for Sarai has never died away.

But the officer said only, "This woman is too beautiful for any but Pharaoh." And he took her and sent her to him.

And since Abram said many times, "She is only my sister," Pharaoh sent him gifts of sheep and oxen and camels and asses, and many slaves, and took Sarai into his bed-chamber (for she said, as Abram told her, "He is my brother only.").

But when Pharaoh tried to touch her, God heard her inward cry and sent an angel to strike his hand away. All through that night Pharaoh tried to touch her, to hold her; and he could not. And when the dawn came, though he longed for her, he had still not touched her, still not held her. And he was perplexed and amazed. And in that morning, all the people of Egypt were struck with a plague, and cried and lamented to one another in the streets and in the houses.

Then at last did Sarai say, "Abram is my husband." And Pharaoh cried out, and called Abram.

And he cried to Abram, "What is this you have done to me? Why did you say 'She is my sister', so that I took her to be mine? Now all my people are afflicted! Take her, and go your way!"

And he sent Sarai back to Abram, so that immediately the plague was lifted. And he did not claim back his gifts, but even added to them. And among them was a bond-maid named Hagar, whom he gave to Sarai for her own. And some say she was his own daughter.

And at his command, for he was afraid and did not wish them to linger, his servants escorted them safely and rapidly out of the land of Egypt. And they brought them into Canaan with their gifts, and left them there.

And this was the land God had told Abram would be his. "Lift up your eyes," God had said, "and look from the place where you are, northward and southward and eastward and westward. There is a land flowing with milk and honey, and unto you will I give it, and to all your generations for ever and ever. And they shall be as many as the specks of dust on the earth, or stars in the sky." And Abram believed, and longed for it.

THE BATTLE OF THE KINGS

Now Abram stood in the land of Canaan, the land of milk and honey where God had promised him he would become a great nation like the stars that sprinkle the night-time sky. And because of Sarai's beauty, he now had sheep and oxen, asses and cattle, and all manner of golden gifts.

And it came to pass so many were their animals, that the herdsmen of Abram and Lot quarrelled, for they took each other's pastureland. And at last Abram said to Lot, "You and I are brothers. Let there be no strife between us. If you be in danger, I will haste to your side, and in all things I will be with you. But separate yourself, I pray you, from me. If you will take the left hand, I will go to the right. If you wish the right, I will go to the left. For is not the whole land before us?"

And Lot lifted up his eyes and beheld all the plain of the Jordan, that it was rich and fertile and well-watered, and it was like God's own garden where Adam and Eve and God had walked, talking together as friends.

So Lot chose him the Plain of the Jordan, and he moved his tent to Sodom. But Abram stayed in the land of Canaan. For God had promised it to him.

Now this was the time when the King of Sodom went to war. For there were then many kings, and many kings together are like proud beasts with haughty necks, that toss their heads and thrust against each other and clash their horns. So nine kings went to war together, five of them against four others, together with all their hosts. And one of the five was the King of Sodom where Lot now lived.

And helping the five were the Devastators, the Giants, whom some call The Busy Ones. For giants still walked the earth in those days. Each was as tall as a cedar tree, and their stride was three miles long, and their shadow when it fell across the path at eventide froze to death any form it touched. Og was one of them, he who had escaped from the Flood on the back of a unicorn in the time when God unplugged the stars. He muttered and roared with the Devastators and the five Kings, and boasted of what he would do with but one little finger if he so minded.

The four Kings with whom they fought had no giants to lend them might. But they had might of their own, for one was Nimrod, Nimrod Amraphel, he of the five thrones piled one above the other, who had pursued Abram many years because of the doom of a dream, and who was one of the ten mightiest Kings in the world.

And these four smote the five Kings like a storm that smashes down the trees and tears them from the ground. And like the raging wind they drove them and their giants and their armies into the slime pits, that lie in the deep, deep valley of the Dead Sea, where the blue unmoving waters lie as deep below as the sky above, and the mists rise up to the mountains like the souls of those who have slipped on the slimy rocks. And they tried to crawl out of the thick yellow water, subduing the haste of their terror lest they plunge even deeper. And those who at last scrambled out fled in fear into the mountains.

But the King of Sodom slithered and slipped in the wet clay, always straining towards the edge and always slipping back, and he cried out aloud for he thought to die. And while he cried out aloud and none paid him heed, the four

Kings and their hosts turned back from their pursuing and took all his kingdom and many captives, and Lot was among them.

Now Og by his strength and his cunning and the length of his stride escaped from the battle, and he fled to Abram and told him in feigned friendship what had befallen. For it is said in song and story that he knew Abram would hasten to rescue Lot, whom he loved above all, and then, he thought, he, Og, would seize the beautiful Sarai for himself, Sarai of the black hair that gleamed like a raven's wing. But she was wise and this did not come about.

When he knew Lot had been captured, Abram seized the sapphire Staff, and it became for him a flaming Sword as it had done for Methuselah. And he called three hundred and eighteen men of his household, all tried and valiant; and at his side strode Eliezer of Damascus, the mighty giant slave whom Nimrod had once given him (who, it was said in song and story was to fell in the battle to come more men than did all the three hundred and eighteen men of his household together). And the battle raged.

But the spears that were savagely hurled at Abram turned into handfuls of earth. And the arrows that leaped at him, turned into chaff that blew away in the wind. But when he stooped and picked up the earth and threw it back, the grains became again hundreds of piercing spears. And he threw back the chaff, and again it became showers of arrows.

And the hosts of the Kings, even Nimrod Amraphel, saw and were afraid. And Nimrod remembered how it had been years ago, when he threw Abram into a blazing furnace that was a wall of golden flame, and how the furnace became a pleasure garden of golden lilies where Abram strolled at ease and smiled to Nimrod.

So Abram conquered all the Kings, even Nimrod Amraphel. And the dream of the comet that swallowed the brilliant stars had come to pass.

All this long while, the king of Sodom had struggled in the pit of clay. Now at last he pulled himself out from the slime and staggered forth to meet Abram. And he said to him, "Keep the goods for yourself. Only give me back the people."

But Abram said, "I do not want your goods. My God is the maker of heaven and earth, and I have sworn to him that I will not take a thread nor a shoe-latchet nor aught that is yours. I have come only to rescue Lot and his household. That is all I have done battle for." And the King of Sodom was astonished.

And now, walking towards him, came the King of Salem, another of those whom Abram had conquered and whose men he had slain. And Abram recognised him. "I have known this man long ago," he said to himself. And outward he said, "It is Shem, walking the earth with a different name, in a different form." For so men did in those days, spanning hundreds of years with a quest that they must keep. (And not only men, but women also though more secretly. Solomon was not yet born, but was he not to say that the Queen of Sheba whom he commanded to appear before him and who left him, was Lilith of the untamed hair who had left Adam when the world was first made?)

And Abram said again to himself, "This is Shem, Shem who was dear to me, in whose house I hid when Nimrod sought my life, Shem who loved me and taught me the words of the stars and the paths of the winds, and gave me the sapphire Staff. Yet today I have raised that Staff against his grandchildren."

And Shem also walked towards him, and said to himself, "This is the young man I knew and loved hundreds of years ago. Yet my own grandchildren have taken captive his kinsfolk, and harmed them sorely." And they were both troubled.

But they met and they embraced, and now there was no anger nor grief between them, but it was once again as it had been in the days long ago. And Shem gave Abram bread and wine, and to all his men also; and they did eat and drink and refreshed themselves and rejoiced together.

And as Abram stood up to depart with Sarai back to the land of Canaan, Shem gave him at last the Book of All Knowledge that had within it the thoughts of the rain and the song of the sun and many wonders beside, as he had long ago given him the sapphire Sword; for he was still roaming the earth and seeking the one who awaited it, and now he had found him. And Abram returned to Canaan. But Lot stayed in Sodom, for that he had chosen.

THE DOOMED CITY

Now Sarai's hair was still black and glossy as a raven's wing, and she was still lovely beyond all others then living.

But she had no children, and she was past the ways of women, being seventy-six years old. Yet God had said to Abram, "As many as the myriad stars in the sky shall your children and your grandchildren be."

So because God had promised this to Abram, and because, after the time of Lilith and of Eve, women now thought more of men than of themselves, she said to Abram, "It may be that I must obtain a child through Hagar whom Pharaoh gave to me." For Hagar was her bond-maid, her slave. And Abram hearkened to her voice; and Hagar conceived, and was with his child.

Now when Hagar saw that she was with child, she despised her mistress. For now she forgot she was a slave, who had been made a slave by her own father, and she remembered that she was the daughter of Pharaoh, and that she carried within her Abram's child. And she walked serenely, her mouth slightly curved in a smile, and she mocked Sarai.

And Sarai said to Abram, "It was I who gave her to you! It was I who made her radiant! And now am I despised!"

And Abram said, "She is a slave. She is in your hand. Do to her what you will."

Then Sarai dealt harshly with her. And it was with Hagar as if she had been caught up by a whirling wind. And she fled from Sarai into the wilderness. And a messenger of God found her like a sparrow on a rooftop, crying by a fountain of water.

And he questioned her softly, and quieted her. And he said to her, "Go back. You shall have a son. And no stranger shall rule over him. He shall be free, rejoicing in the wilderness. And God shall make of him a great nation." And you shall call him Ishmael, for 'Ishmael' means 'God has heard'.

And she was sick and sad in her slavery, and she listened. So she returned. And Ishmael was born.

And Ishmael grew to be a youth. But Sarai was still without child of her own. Then it was that God said to Abram, "Now will I give you a son of Sarai."

And Abram laughed. In his heart he said, "Shall a son be born unto one that is a hundred years old? And shall Sara, that is ninety years old, have a child?" And he had Ishmael already and loved him, so he said aloud, "But what of the child I have?"

And God said, "Did I not hear Ishmael, and the voice of his mother? Twelve princes shall come of him. And he shall be a great nation, for the generations that come from him will be numberless.

"But I am making this covenant with the child of Abram and Sarai, that is yet to be born. And that child you shall call Isaac, because you laughed at my promise." For Isaac means 'laughter'.

And so that they were ready for whatever magnificent thing might befall, God changed their names to Sarah and Abraham, so that she was no more called 'My Princess' but 'Princess of All', and he was no more called 'Great Father' but was 'Father of a Multitude of Nations'. But Abram did not straightway tell this to Sarai, for he was still touched with doubt and laughter, and thinking Sarai would laugh also.

Now the day was hot, and Abram sat in the tent door. And he saw three men approaching, strangers to him, and wayfarers, and he thought they must be weary. And he ran to meet them. And he bowed down to the earth, and said, "Rest a little. Let now some water be fetched to wash your feet. And you will recline under the tree, and I will fetch a morsel of bread to strengthen your heart. And after that you shall move on."

And he hastened to the tent and bade Sarai make cakes, and he ran to the herd and took a calf, tender and good, and gave it to the servants to make ready, and he took also curds and milk and set them before them; and he stood by them under the tree while they did eat. And one of them said to him, "Sarah, your wife, shall have a son."

Now Sarah heard. For she was in her tent door, and behind the stranger. And she had never yet heard herself called Sarah, Princess of All. And she laughed within herself, being now very old and her husband also. And the stranger said, "Why did Sarah laugh? Is anything too hard for the Maker of Heaven and Earth?" And she was afraid – for she was within her tent, and he could not see her, and did not know her.

And she said softly, under her breath, "I laughed not."

And he answered from where he was, "Nay, but you did."

Then the three strangers rose, to go on their journey. And Abraham went with them a little way, as was the custom. And Abraham had not thought they were angels, since they seemed to eat the food of men (for it is said that angels, being made of air or fire, eat only the smell of fire or the fumes of water. Yet sometimes it is known they dissemble.)

And as they walked, God said softly, "He has given my angels food and drink, and made them welcome. Shall I hide from him that which I am doing? Shall I not tell him that they have errands, one to bring news of the child to come, one to destroy Sodom, and one to save Lot?"

So God said, "Abraham, there is weeping in Sodom. There are voices continually weeping. I am going to see who it is who cries. Then will I do what must be done, that the weeping may cease."

And Abraham saw that the messenger who had brought news of the child's coming now moved away, and the two who were left turned towards Sodom. And he stood quite still. For Abraham had studied the Book of All Knowledge that is Worth Knowing, and he knew the signs of calamity and mourning. And he had heard of the evils that were done in Sodom. And he knew Sodom was doomed.

And he said to God, "Will you then indeed sweep away the righteous with the wicked? Perhaps there are fifty righteous within the city. Will you indeed sweep the city away, and not forgive it for the fifty righteous that are there? That be far from you to do after this manner – to slay the righteous with the wicked. That be far from you."

And God heard his reproach and said, "If I find in Sodom fifty righteous men, then will I forgive the whole place for their sake."

But Abraham said further, "I am but dust and ashes that dare argue with you, God. But if there are five short of fifty righteous? Will you destroy the city for lack of that five?"

And God answered him, "I will not destroy it if I find there forty-five righteous."

Then Abraham said, "Perhaps there shall be only forty."

And God answered, "I will not do it, if there are forty."

And Abraham said, "O let not God be angry. But perhaps there will be thirty."

And God told him, "I will not destroy it, if there be thirty."

And Abraham said, "I have taken it on me to speak – perhaps there shall be twenty."

And God said, "I will not destroy it, for the twenty's sake."

And Abraham said, "O let not the Almighty be angry, and I will speak only this once more. Perhaps ten shall be found there."

And God said, "I will not destroy it, for the ten's sake."

Then God left Abraham. And the two messengers who had been waiting outside the walls of Sodom till Abraham had finished his bargaining with God, entered the city.

Now Lot sat in the gate of the city, and it was eventide. And he rose up to meet the two strangers. And bowing down to the ground, for he took them for travellers, he said, "Pray turn aside, my lords, and wash your feet, and tarry all night in my house. Then go you on your way in the morning."

And they answered him, "Trouble yourself not. We will lie in the street all night."

Now there were beds in the street for strangers, and if any stranger lay on one, the people of Sodom would surround him, and if he were shorter than the bed they would seize his arms and legs and pull them, till his body separated, and he died. And if he were too long for the bed, they would lift axes, and cleave his head and his limbs.

But Lot urged them into his house, and he locked the door. And he baked for them, and he made them a feast. But before they had lain down to rest, the people of Sodom surrounded the house, all the people from every quarter both young and old, and they shouted to Lot, "Where are the strangers that came to you last night? Bring them forth!"

Now Sodom was one of the richest of all nations, for gold grew beneath the roots of their pot-herbs, and diamonds and pearls under the harvested corn. Yet it was Sodomite law, not to give even a crumb of bread to a stranger. Whoever in Sodom offered a stranger food was burned alive, while the stranger was robbed of all he had, and flung naked outside the city gates. Had this not been done to Lot's eldest daughter when first he came to the city, that she gave water to an old man who entered the gates, and they seized her and burned her alive?

And Lot went out to them, locking the door again behind him, and he said, "I pray you, do not harm my guests. Let me send out my two young daughters instead, and do to them what you will. But these men are in the shelter of my home." For in those days - so long after Lilith the proud, the strong, the golden-haired - women were of little account even to men deemed righteous. (But there are those who believe Lilith will return. That is another story.)

But they cried, "Stand back! You who do not belong, who came only to sojourn for a while, dare you to tell us what to do! Beware, lest we do to you worse even than we do to them!"

And they thrust him aside, and began to batter the wall down. But the strangers unlocked the door, and drew him back in, and locked it again behind him. And they smote the people at the door of the house, both young and old, with blindness, so that they wearied themselves trying to find the door.

Then said the strangers in the house to Lot, "Have you any here besides? Sons and daughters and sons-in-law, and whomever you have in the city - bring them out of this place, for God has sent us to destroy it, for the crying herein is loud."

And Lot went out and spoke to his sons-in-law that had married his daughters, and he said, "Come you out of this place, for God will destroy the city!" But he seemed to them as one that jested, and they laughed. And there were not ten to hear him.

Then at the first gleam of sunrise the strangers hastened Lot, saying, "Take your wife and your two daughters that are here, and go, lest you also be swept away!" But still he lingered, till they caught him by the hand, and also his wife and his two daughters, and they dragged them forth all the way, till they were outside the city. And one said, "Escape for your life! Look not behind you, neither stay in any of the Plain! Look not behind you, lest you be swept away!"

And Lot cried, "No, I cannot. I cannot escape to the mountain, lest the evil overtake me and I die. But there is a little city nearby, a very little city, a little one which perhaps you will not destroy - oh let me escape there, and spare it for me, for it is oh so little."

And the stranger said, "I have accepted this from you too, that I will save this little city. Only hasten!"

And as the sun rose, and Lot and his family drew near the little city, an East wind blew. And blazing fire and brimstone rained upon Sodom, and all the cities of the

Plain were destroyed, together with their people and their beasts, save only the very little city that Lot had spoken for.

But as they entered the little city, Lot's wife turned to look behind her, for she did not know if her daughters were safely following, and she was afraid for them. And the evil caught her. And she became a rock of salt, and was held there for ever.

And Abraham rose early as the day dawned, and he stood in the place where he had bargained with God. And he looked out to see if there had been enough righteous men to save the city. But the smoke of the land went up to him as the smoke of a furnace. And all he saw was a woman of salt wreathed in the mist of the Dead Sea.

The World Laughing

So the world grew further and further away from the Man-and-Woman-made-all-in-one, and the days of the Garden of Delight where humans, beasts and birds had spoken the same language.

And now God had destroyed the world once by water, and once by fire, as Seth had read in the Book of All Knowledge Worth Knowing, when he built his towers. And a woman of salt stood by the Dead Sea. (And travellers say she still stands there today, caught and held by the evil on the shore, still looking back to a ghostly burnt-out city; while over the water, untouched, stands a small town, still called Zoar, 'the little one'.)

But Lot had escaped from death; for Abraham cared for him, and twice rescued him (while twice he handed over Sarah; for after the burning of Sodom, he let yet another king take her, saying again, "She is only my sister." But that is another story).

Now on the day foretold by the stranger, Sarah gave birth to a child; and he was called Isaac, for Abraham and Sarah had both laughed in turn. And when the child was weaned, Abraham gave a great feast, and to this came Og the giant, who had often taunted Abraham, saying, "Still no child?"

And the guests laughed at Og, and said, "What say you now?"

And Og snarled, "I could kill the child with the tip of one finger!" For he cared not what he had promised Noah in the days of the deluge.

Now when Isaac was born, Sarah was confused, being

so old, and said, "Now the whole world will laugh." And when she saw the lad Ishmael at the weaning feast, playing with the baby Isaac and laughing with him, she said to Abraham, "Ishmael laughs at our son, and mocks us."

And she said, "Cast him out, him and his mother. Why should the son of a slave be with Isaac, our very own child, and laugh!"

Now this was grievous to Abraham for Ishmael was his son. Yet he was not a man to argue, except for Lot's sake when he even argued with the Maker of Heaven and Earth. And he rose up early in the morning, and took bread and a bottle of water and put it on Hagar's shoulder and sent her away, her and the lad also, his first child.

And Hagar wandered in the wilderness of Beersheba. And the sun was hot and the water was spent, and her mouth was wet only with tears. And she left Ishmael under one of the shrubs, and went and sat down a full bowshot away, for she said, "Let me not see him die." And she wept.

And God heard her weeping and heard the cracked, hoarse voice of the lad, and she called to her, "What ails you, Hagar? Fear not. God hears the voice of Ishmael. Lift him up, hold him fast by the hand. Did I not say I will make of him a great nation?"

And God opened her eyes. And nearby was a well of water. She filled the bottle with water, and she gave it to Ishmael, and took his hand. And he drank. And she drank also. And they were refreshed, and they sighed, and drank again. And they looked at one another with pleasure.

And they stayed in the wilderness of Paran, and dwelt there. And Ishmael grew, and became a great hunter and an archer. And he was the very first of the Arabs whom God made a great nation.

Now it is said in song and story that Abraham began to long for him, for his son Ishmael. And after many years he made ready his camel to journey to him.

Then Sarah beseeched him, for she feared she would lose him. "Stay my lord, stay!" And when he would not hearken, she said, "Swear you will not alight from your camel when you reach his tent, lest you cleave to him, and forget Isaac!" So he swore it to her, and he went.

So rode he into the wilderness of Paran, where Ishmael dwelt. And when he reached the tent, Ishmael was away hunting. And Abraham kept his pledge to Sarah, and did not alight from the camel, but called to Ishmael's wife, for she stood at the tent door with many children. "Give me refreshment, daughter, for I am faint from travelling."

But she did not move towards him, nor bring him water to drink, nor did she look at him, nor ask his name, but only reviled her husband and her children. Then Abraham said, "When your husband returns, tell him an aged man of such and such a look came in search of him. Tell him you did not ask his name, but that he said to you, 'Tell your husband to cast away his tent-peg, and cut himself another.'" And Abraham rode away.

Then Ishmael returned from hunting and his wife gave him the message. And Ishmael understood it. And he sent away the wife who would not bring an old man water in the heat of the day, and he took him another.

Now when three years had passed, Abraham came again. And again he remained seated on his camel for he had pledged it to Sarah, and he enquired again for Ishmael.

And the new wife said to him, "Come in. Take

refreshment, and wash your feet, for you must be weary and faint from travelling."

And he answered, "I cannot dismount, daughter, for I have given a promise. But bring me water to quench my thirst, I pray you."

"That will I do gladly, and bread and fresh goat's milk besides," she said. And she did so.

And Abraham said to her, "When your husband returns, daughter, tell him an aged man of such and such a look came in search of him. And that he said to you, 'Tell your husband that his new tent-peg is an excellent one, and he should take good care of it.'"

And when Ishmael returned from hunting, she told him of the man, and he understood and rejoiced that she had cared for his father. And he took her and his children to visit Abraham, in the land of Canaan, and they dwelt there together many days. And Isaac and Ishmael were brothers, Isaac the rock-dove that seeks a home, Ishmael the wandering turtle-dove.

And it is said in song and story that on that day Ishmael looked with wonder at the face of Isaac, and at the face of Abraham, and at the face of Isaac again, for it was the same face. And this was how it came about. When Isaac was born and Sarah said, "The whole world will laugh!" the world did laugh. And they said in their laughter and their whisperings that Sarah and Abraham had sent to buy the child in the market-place, for it could not possibly be theirs.

And God heard their laughter and their whisperings. So she put forth a hand, and touched the infant on the cheek. And the face of the child changed and it became entirely the face of Abraham, only smaller; and the mouths of gossiping people were immediately shut. So it was that when Ishmael saw his father and brother again he gazed with wonder at them both.

But as years passed, and the child grew into a man, and none could tell Isaac from Abraham, all were forever confused. So God decided to make an end to it, and he put forth a hand and turned Abraham's hair white, to mark the difference.

Till then, none had grown old, save in years. But from then on, age showed in face and body; and men were seen to be older men than their sons, and women were seen to be older than their daughters. And it was easy to distinguish them. And so it has been ever since.

THE SLAVE'S WOOING

Now it came to pass that Sarah died, being one hundred years, seven and twenty. And her hair was still as black and glossy as a raven's wing. And Abraham and Isaac mourned for her.

Now Abraham was old and well-stricken in years. And God had promised Abraham that generations would spring from him as countless as the dust on the earth or the stars in the sky, to inherit the land of Canaan. And now he had a child, but no grandchild. For Isaac, his son, only mourned for Sarah.

Then Abraham said to Eliezer of Damascus, who was his servant, "Go to my country, to my kindred who are there, and find a wife for my son. And bring her back to the land of Canaan."

And Eliezer said, "But if the woman will not be willing to return with me into this land, what shall I do then? Shall I take your son to her, to the land whence you came?"

And Abraham said, "No. That is not the promise. The God of Heaven took me from my father's house and the land of my nativity, and brought me here. And God swore to me, 'Unto you and to your generations will I give this land.'

"God will send an angel before you to prosper you, that you might find the one that is chosen. If she be not willing to follow you, then shall you be free of this oath. But you shall not take my son back thither, for this is the land that is promised him."

So Eliezer made ready ten camels, and many armed retainers, and asses, laden with gold and silver, with jewels and silks, and all goodly things of his master; and he rode with his caravan to the city of Nakos that lies between two rivers.

And outside the city he made the camels lie down by the well, at the time when women go forth to draw water. And he said in his heart, "O God of my master, send me good speed this day, and prosper my journey. Behold, I stand by the fountain of water, and the daughters of the men of the city come forth. Let it come to pass, that the damsel to whom I shall say 'Let down your pitcher, that I may drink' and she answers 'Drink, and let your camels drink also,' let she be the one you have chosen in wisdom for my master's son."

And before he had done speaking in his heart, Rebekah came out, with a pitcher on her shoulder. And she was young and very fair to look upon. And she went down to the fountain and filled her pitcher, and started back again.

And Eliezer ran to meet her, and said, "Give me to drink a little, I pray you."

And she said, "Drink, my lord." And quickly she let down the pitcher into her hand that he might refresh himself. And when he had drunk as much as he wished, she said, "And let your camels drink also." And she quickly emptied her pitcher into the trough, and ran again to the well for more water; and she drew water for all his camels.

Then Eliezer looked long and steadfastly upon her. And as the camels had done drinking, he took a golden ring, and two gold bracelets from the goodly things of Abraham that he had brought.

And he said, "Tell me, I pray you, whose daughter are you?"

And she answered, "I am Rebekah, the daughter of

Bethuel, Nahor's son." And Nahor was the brother of Abraham.

Then did Eliezer give her the ring. And he put the bracelets on her hands. And he said, "Is there room in the house of your father where we might lodge?"

And she answered, "We have both straw and food enough, and room to lodge also."

Now Rebekah ran and told her mother of the happenings. And Rebekah had a brother, Laban. And when Laban heard his sister say, "Thus spoke the man unto me," and he saw the ring and the bracelets on his sister's hand, he ran out to the man, who still stood by the camels at the fountain. And he said, "Come in! Why do you stand outside? Come in!"

Then Eliezer came into the house, and Laban untied the camels, and gave them water and provender, and he brought water to wash Eliezer's feet and the feet of all men with him. And he set food before him to eat.

But Eliezer said, "I will not eat till I have told my errand."

And Laban said, "Speak on."

And Eliezer said, "I am Abraham's servant. And the Maker of Heaven and Earth has blessed Abraham exceedingly, and has given him flocks and herds, and silver and gold, and men-servants and maid-servants, and camels and asses. And he is become great.

"And Sarah, my master's wife, bore a son to my master when she was old; and unto him he has given all he has. And my master said to me, 'You shall not take a wife for my son from the daughters of the Canaanites, in whose land I dwell. But you shall go to my father's house, and to my kindred, and take from there a wife for my son, and bring her back to this land.'

"And I said to my master, 'But if the woman will not follow me?' And he said, 'The God of Heaven before whom I walk will prosper your way.'

"So I came this day to the fountain, and said, 'Oh God of my master Abraham, prosper the way which I go. Here I stand by the fountain of water. Let it come to pass that the maiden that comes forth to draw water, to whom I shall say "Give me, I pray, a little water to drink," and she shall say "Drink, and I will give your camels to drink also"– let that one be the woman the God of my master has chosen.'

"And scarce had I done speaking in my heart, then Rebekah came forth with her pitcher on her shoulder. And she went down to the fountain and drew water. And I said to her, 'Let me drink, I pray you.' And she made haste and let down her pitcher from her shoulder, and said, 'Drink. And I will give your camels drink also.' So I drank, and the camels drank.

"And I asked her, ' Whose daughter are you?' And she answered, 'The daughter of Bethuel, Nahor's son.' And Nahor is my master's brother. So I gave to her the ring. And I put the bracelets on her hands, and I bowed my head, and thanked the God of my master Abraham that he had led me in the right way.

"And now, if you will deal kindly and truly with my master, tell me."

Then Bethuel, Rebekah's father, and Laban her brother, answered him, "We cannot speak either good or bad of it. It is decreed. Take her."

And Eliezer bowed himself down to the earth. And he brought forth jewels of silver and of gold, and he brought forth bales of silk, and he gave them to Rebekah. And he gave to her brother and her mother most precious things. And they did eat and drink, he and the men with him, and they tarried all night.

And when they arose in the morning, Eliezer said, "Send me away to my master."

But they said, "Wait a little. Let the damsel stay with us awhile."

And he said, "Delay me not."

So they said, "We will send for the damsel and enquire at her own mouth." And they called her, and said to her, "Will you go?"

And she said, "I will."

Then said they to her, "May you be the mother of thousands of ten thousands." And they sent her away, with her nurse (for she was young) and with her damsels; and she went with Abraham's servant and his men. (And it is said for this, and the many other loyal services Eliezer did for Abraham, Abraham freed him, and he became himself a king. But that is a later story.)

And as Rebekah rode upon the camel with Eliezer at her side, it was evening, and the shadows were lengthening, and the low sun blinded their eyes. And Isaac walked out to meditate in the fields. For he had come from Hagar's well, where the angel had once found Hagar when Sarah had sent her away in anger; for it was a still and silent place, that gave him comfort.

And Rebekah said to Eliezer, "What man is this who walks in the field to meet us?"

And he said, "It is my master's son."

And Eliezer told Isaac how he had met Rebekah at the

well, and he told him all the things that had come to pass. And Isaac took her and loved her. And she was sweeter than honey and the honeycomb to him. And he was at last comforted for Sarah, his mother.

THE FIRST CHEATING

So it came to pass that Rebekah left her brother Laban, and her father and mother, and rode with Eliezer of Damascus back to the land of Canaan.

Now Rebekah was very young, and for a long time she had no children. But after many years, she conceived. And they were two twin children. And they fought within her, moving so strongly their elbows, their fists, their feet, that she said to God, "Is it always thus with women?" For she did not know, having now no mother, and the mother of Isaac being dead.

And God said to her, "It is because there are two nations warring within you. One shall be stronger than the other. And the other shall serve him."

Now when the children were born, the first-born had much hair of reddish-gold. And him they called Esau, which means 'well-formed'. But the second one was hairless. (And indeed it is said today that it is his hairless face that is imprinted on the moon.) Him they called Jacob, which means 'one who snatches another's place' or 'cheater'; for when they were born, and came forth one after the other, the second had hold of his brother's heel, as if he strove with him for the first place.

Now Abraham had given to Isaac the sapphire Staff that is also a Sword, with which he had smitten four kings, and the Book of All Knowledge Worth Knowing, which he had had from Seth on that very same day. And when the time came, Isaac gave them to Esau, for he was the elder and his well-beloved.

And because of the Book, Esau knew the sighing

thoughts of the rain, and the crying and the calling of the animals and birds. And with the Staff that was a Sword he brought in meat that was food for his family; for by now men were lords over animals. And his father Isaac ate of his venison, and admired and loved him. But Jacob was a quiet man, living in tents as a shepherd. And his mother loved Jacob.

And some say, when Esau was hunting in the forest he came by chance on King Nimrod, he who had the Cloak; and they fought a mighty battle. And Esau vanquished Nimrod and retrieved from him the Cloak that had been stolen from Noah on the day he opened the skylight of the Ark. But some say that Isaac himself gave the Cloak to Esau, that it had already been retrieved from Nimrod, and that with his own hands Isaac gave it to Esau whom he loved.

The songs and the stories have diverse words, but all say the Three Gifts, once separated, now came to Esau. And with them he walked in the universe and knew animal, bird, and fish, and the rulers of the sky, and many mysteries.

Now it happened one day when Jacob was stirring a pottage of red lentils, that Esau came in from the fields, being tired and hungry, and lifted his face to the smell of the pottage, and said, "Let me swallow, I pray you, some of that red, red pottage. So faint am I from hunger."

And Jacob said, "Sell me first your birthright."

And Esau said, "I am tired and hungry. What is this talk of birthrights?"

And Jacob said again, "Give me your birthright, for this pottage."

And Esau said, "Behold, I am at the point to die. What profit shall the birthright do to me?"

And Jacob said, "Swear it to me first." So he swore to him, selling him his birthright. Then Jacob gave him bread, and pottage of red lentils, and he ate and drank and was strengthened, and rose up and went his way, thinking no more of it.

Now as the years went by, Isaac their father grew possessed of many flocks and herds, and of many wells of living water, and of a great household, so that the other peoples envied him. But he made a covenant with them, that in his might he would do them no hurt since they had never done him hurt, but would rather befriend them. And he made them a great feast, and they ate and drank together and departed from him in peace. And so it was that the life of Isaac was honourable and blessed and peaceful.

And it came to pass that when he was old, and his eyes were dim so that he could no longer see clearly, he called to Esau his elder son whom he loved, saying, "My son." And Esau answered, "Here am I."

And Isaac said, "Behold now, I am already old. Who can know now the day of his death? Therefore take, I pray you, your quiver and your bow, and go out to the field, and hunt for me wild game and make me savoury food such as I do love, and bring it to me. And I will eat of the venison, and give you now my blessing, before the time I die." So Esau went out into the field.

But Rebekah, their mother, heard the words of Isaac. And she said to Jacob, "Behold, I heard your father speak to Esau, your brother, saying, 'Bring me venison and make me savoury food, that I may eat and bless you before the time I die.' Now hearken, my son, to my voice, and do what I command you.

"Go you to the flock, and bring me two good kids of the goats. And I will make them savoury food for your father, tasting like the venison of Esau such as he loves. And you shall bring it to him, that he may eat, and bless you instead."

And Jacob said, "But my father will know me if he touch me. For my skin is smooth, and not like Esau's. And I shall seem to him a mocker, and I shall bring a curse on me, not a blessing."

But his mother said, "Fear not. I will take the curse, if curse there be. Only do as I tell you."

So he did as she said. And his mother made savoury food such as his father loved. And she took the garments of Esau which he had left in the house, even the Cloak which Adam and Eve had brought from Eden, and she put it upon her younger son. And she put the hairy skins of the goats over his hands and the smooth of his neck. And she put the savoury dish with bread into one hand of Jacob, and into the other the Staff of Esau which long long ago was Adam's.

And he came upon his father, and said, "My father."

And Isaac said, "Here am I. Who are you, my son?"

And Jacob said, "I am Esau. I have done your bidding. Now eat of my venison, that you may bless me."

And Isaac said, perplexed, "How is it you have found it so quickly my son?"

And he said, "God sent me good speed."

And Isaac, being still puzzled, said, "Come here, I pray you, that I may touch you, my son, to know whether you be my very son Esau or not."

And he came near. And Isaac touched his hands, and said, "The voice is the voice of Jacob. But the hands are the hands of Esau." And he said again wonderingly, "Are you my very son Esau?"

And Jacob said, "I am."

Then did he say, "Bring the dish near, that I may eat of my son's venison." And he brought the goat's meat near to him, and he did eat, and he brought him wine also and he drank.

Then his father Isaac said to him, "Come near now and kiss me, my son." And he came near and kissed him. And his father smelled the smell of his Cloak which was Esau's, and it smelled of a field which the Maker had blessed, a field with apple trees and strong-smelling spices. And he smelled his Staff that still smelled sweetly of the Garden of Eden. And he said, "This is indeed the goodly smell of Esau."

So he blessed him, saying, "God give you of the dew of heaven, and plenty of corn and wine. Peoples shall serve you, and nations bow down to you. He shall be blessed, who blesses you, and cursed, who curses you. And you shall be lord over your brethren, and your mother's sons shall acknowledge your might."

Scarce had he made an end of blessing Jacob, and Jacob was gone from his presence, than Esau his brother came in from the hunting, for being without his Staff and his Cloak, he was not so swift as of wont. And he quickly made savoury food such as his father loved, for he said of his father, "He is a king in my sight." And he laid it before him, and said, "Let my father rise up, and eat of his son's venison, and give his blessing."

And Isaac said, "Who are you?"

And he said, surprised, "I am your son, your first-born, Esau."

Then Isaac trembled very exceedingly, and said, "Who

then is he that has brought venison before me, so that I did eat of all before you came, and have blessed him?"

Then Esau, hearing the words of his father, cried with an exceeding great and bitter cry, "Bless me also, even me also, oh my father."

And his father said, "Your brother came with cunning, and has taken away your blessing."

And Esau cried, "Is he not rightly named Jacob? For twice he has snatched what is mine. He took away my birthright and I kept silent. And now that he has taken away my blessing shall I still keep silent?" And he cried to his father, "Have you not left a blessing for me?"

And Isaac said in sorrow, "Behold, I have made him lord over you, and all his brethren have I given to him as servants, and with corn and wine have I sustained him. What then shall I do for you, my son, my son?"

And Esau cried, "Have you then only one blessing, my father? Oh, my father, bless me also." And Esau lifted up his voice, and wept.

Then Isaac would have cursed Jacob. But God said to him, "Did you not say to him, 'He shall be cursed who curses you, and blessed who blesses you?'" So Isaac put his hand upon his mouth. And he wept with Esau.

Then Isaac his father said to Esau, "Behold, there is enough of the dew of heaven, and of the fat places of the earth, for you also. But now, by the sword must you live and by the chase. And for that you shall be renowned, and for power of body. But he shall be lord over you. For what is said cannot be unsaid, though one weep."

And Esau hated Jacob, and said that day in his heart, "One day I will kill him."

THE STONE ON THE WELL

Now Jacob, who had cheated his brother and cheated his father, was afraid. He saw the face of Esau. And he cried out to Rebekah, "There is but one step between me and death!"

But Rebekah said, "Esau's anger is a fire of thorns. It flares up in a moment, and in a moment is spent. Get you to my brother's house in Haran. In a few days he will forget. Then shall I send for you again." (She was sure she knew the future. But she knew only part of it. It would be years, not days, not months, till she sent for him.)

Then, not wishing to speak of the cheating, but hearing the crackle of death like warning twigs, she said to Isaac, "I am weary of my life because of the wives of Esau; for they are the daughters of this land, and bitter to me. If Jacob also take a wife of the daughters of this land, what good shall my life do me? It were better to send him to my brother's house to choose a wife of our own kind there."

And he answered wearily, "So be it."

So it was that neither Isaac nor Rebekah spoke of what Jacob had done. But it is said in song and story that Jacob left his home - the home of Isaac, with his flocks and herds and wells of living water - with only one camel, and water in one flask of skin; that he who had always fed delicately from the venison of Esau had to beg or earn his bread along the way to Haran; that he arrived at Laban's house without bride-price, without retinue, without laden asses, without treasure, but near naked and wild. And there was about him a lost air as if he had been caught up by a strong wind and set down elsewhere.

Yet, because of Rebekah, he carried with him the Cloak and the sapphire Staff with which he had deceived Isaac, and the Book of All Knowledge Worth Knowing also. For as he left in haste, she gave them all to him, having taken the Book secretly from Esau's tent. And she whispered, "He that has the birthright and the blessing, must have the Gifts." (And Esau knew not, for he had rushed away from the house, lest he strike in front of his father).

Now it came to pass that as Jacob came with his one camel to the city of Luz, the sun was setting. And he was now famished, and poor, and unkempt and weary, so that he said angrily, "Who would think that the child of Isaac would be a vagabond, and dare not enter the gates for his raggedness." So in pity for himself he took one of the stones of the place and lay down on the ground to sleep, with the stone beneath his head.

Now this was a place where many stones were the dwelling-place of spirits. And when Jacob laid his head thereon, he dreamed a dream. He saw a ladder set on earth, and the uppermost end touched heaven. And angels went about their work, going up and down the ladder. And a voice in the dream said, "The land whereon you lie, to you I will give it, and to all who have life from you. I will keep you, and bring you back into this land, and never leave you, till all this is done."

Then Jacob awakened out of his sleep and was afraid, and said, "This is the house of God, and I knew it not." (And ever since, Luz has been called Beth-el which means 'The House of God', and all know it by that name.)

And Jacob said, "If the God of the dream will be with me, and will keep me in the way that I go, as the dream did say, and will give me bread to eat and raiment to put on, and bring me back to my father's house in peace, then this shall be the God I will serve."

And making this bargain (though some call it a vow)

Jacob went on his journey.

And Jacob came at last into the land of the people of the east. And before him was a field, with a well from which the sheep were watered. And three flocks of sheep lay by the well. But across it was a huge and mighty stone.

Then Jacob raised up his voice to the shepherds, saying, "Whence come ye?"

"From Haran," they answered him.

"Know you then Laban?" he said.

"We know him. Who would not know Laban? He is not a man who can remain unknown."

"Is it well with him?"

"It is well. See now, the one who comes with his sheep is his daughter Rachel."

Yet Jacob turned not, but continued as was wont with him to busy himself in another's affairs, saying, "It is still high day. The light is not yet spent. Neither is it time for the cattle to be gathered together. Why do you not water the sheep and feed them?"

"We cannot water the sheep," answered the shepherds, "till the many flocks have gathered. We wait for all to come. For then together we roll the stone from the well's mouth. It is a mighty stone, and no one man may move it, nor even three."

As he spoke, Rachel reached the well. Jacob turned and saw her. For seven seconds he looked. And silently he turned back to the well, and straightway rolled away the stone. And the mighty rock fell away as one brushes away a grasshopper.

So he watered her flock. Then he kissed her. "Rachel. My cousin Rachel," he said, and wept. And his love for her was instant, and remained as unfailing as the moon; and all have marvelled at it.

THE FOURTEEN YEARS' WINNING

Now Laban remembered the days gone by. He bethought him of Eliezer of Damascus, the slave who had come from Jacob's father, leading ten laden camels, who had given bracelets and a ring of gold to Rebekah when he met her at the well, and many jewels and raiment of purple silk beside. And to Laban, when he left, he gave all manner of precious things.

But Jacob had come with nothing. His body was bare beneath a dirty cloak, and only a staff saved him from falling. And Laban wondered at his forsakenness.

But he said, "Surely you are my bone and my flesh," and he embraced Jacob (though some say that his hands searched for hidden silks wrapped round his body, and that his tongue as he kissed him slipped between his lips and felt for diamonds carried in his mouth, so that Jacob said wearily, "Uncle, I have nothing.").

And Jacob wept, and said to him, "I came with slaves, with mules, with luscious foods. Would I come to you empty-handed, uncle, brother of my mother? But the son of my brother Esau, whose name is Eliphaz and who is swift in body and in spirit also, and who is jealous that my father loves me, did gather ten of my brother's comrades, and they pursued me, vowing to kill me.

"And when I perceived from a glint at my side that Eliphaz was close beside me, and heard the snorting breath of his horse, I hastily dismounted from my camel and flung myself in the dust, and begged their mercy.

"But he and the men that were with him, even my brother's comrades, took all the treasures I brought you, all the laden asses and the servants and the gold and silver. Even the very silks I wore, all these Eliphaz took, saying proudly, 'These are Esau's. These are my father's.' Only my life Eliphaz left me, and the one camel that I rode upon, and a little water in a flask of skin." And he wept anew.

But Laban smiled with bitterness in his heart, and thought, "I am not a fool. He has done some wrong, and Isaac has cast him out with nothing. And he comes to me. Shall I then have the feeding of him!" and was angry.

Now in those days, many had idols or images whose name was teraphim; and the teraphim whispered at certain times, answering questions, resolving doubts, and foretelling the future. So Laban spoke to his teraphim, saying, "This man who is my sister's son, and has been cast out by his father, comes empty-handed, and expects to eat and drink at my table! And who knows but he may stay for months, peradventure for years!"

And his teraphim whispered to him, "Be careful, for his stars are favourable. Do not offend him, then for his sake, whatever you do, in house or field, will be blessed."

Then said Laban, "But if I suggest he enter my service, may he not ask high wages!"

And the teraphim whispered, "He will demand only women. If he is ever angry, offer another woman, and he will stay."

So it was that Jacob abode with Laban for one month and for that month he served him for naught. And Laban turned the matter over in his mind. Then Laban said to him, "A month is gone. Because you are my kinsman, you need not forever serve me for naught. What shall your wages be?"

And Jacob said, "I will serve you seven years for Rachel."

And Laban smiled in himself, and said aloud, "It is better that I give her to you than that I give her to another man." So Jacob served him seven whole years for Rachel. And they seemed to him but a few days for the love he bore her.

Then did Jacob say, "Give me my wife, for my days are fulfilled." So Laban called all in Padam-Aram to his house for a wedding banquet, and they feasted for one week.

Now Laban had two daughters, Leah the older and Rachel the younger, and both were beautiful. But Leah's eyes were not as bright as Rachel's. And Jacob loved Rachel.

And Rachel said to Jacob, "Beware my father, for he can deceive."

And Jacob said, "I also."

Then Rachel said, "I fear he will order my sister to take my place in the wedding chamber. For here no man enjoys his wife by sunlight nor by candlelight, but by darkness only."

"Then will we have a sign," said Jacob. "If it be truly you, my own Rachel, touch you first the great toe of my right foot, and then my right thumb and then the very tip of my right ear. So shall I know you."

And she said, "I will remember."

Now it came to pass that as the wedding guests were feasting, Laban ordered Leah to enter the darkness of the wedding chamber. And Rachel's heart trembled for herself and Jacob, and for her sister, for Leah would have been shamed, knowing not the signs. For though Rachel loved Jacob, she loved Leah also. So she wept and revealed the signs to her.

So it came that in the night, Jacob said, "Rachel? Are you Rachel?"

And Leah answered, "Here am I." And she performed the signs, and they lay together.

But in the pale light of dawn, Jacob saw her, that she was Leah. And he cried out, "Deceiver! And daughter of deceiver! In the night I said, 'Rachel, Rachel', and you came to me!"

And Leah said sadly, "And your father said, 'Esau, Esau' and you came to him."

Then did Jacob cry with anger to Laban, "What is this you have done to me? Did I not serve with you for Rachel? Why then have you beguiled me?"

And Laban answered calmly, "It is not so done here that the younger pushes before the older." And Jacob pressed down his anger.

Then Laban remembered again the words of the teraphim, and he said, "Rachel too you shall have, after this one week of rejoicing. But you must serve me further another seven years." And Jacob, submitting himself, did so. For he loved her, and she was very dear to him.

THE MOTTLING

In the house of Laban, whence Jacob had fled after robbing Esau and betraying his father, the teraphim had whispered, "Give him women, and he will stay." And Laban had given him Leah and Rachel and their two handmaids beside. For in those days men had many wives. But of all of them he loved Rachel best.

Now after seven years he had ten sons and one daughter. (And of that one daughter there is a blood-soaked story that is not told here.) But still he had no child from Rachel, and the two lamented.

Then God remembered Rachel, and hearkened to her crying; and God gave her a child. And Rachel called him Joseph which means 'My sadness is taken away'.

And it came to pass, that on that very day that Joseph was born, Rebekah at last sent for Jacob, through her old nurse, she who came with her when Rebekah rode as a bride with Eliezer in time gone by. And it was fourteen years since Rebekah had whispered to Jacob, "Stay but a few days with my brother, till Esau's anger dies away. Then will I send for you."

And Jacob said to Laban, "My second seven years is ended. Now will I go to my own place, and to my country. Give me my wives and my children for whom I have served you, and let me go."

And Laban said, "Stay, and I will give you whatever wages you ask. Tell me, and I will give them."

Then did Jacob think to put off his going. And he answered, "You know that I served you for Leah and Rachel. And have not your cattle fared well with me? For it was little you had before I came, and it has increased abundantly; and God has blessed you wherever I set my foot. And now shall I not provide for my own household?"

And Laban said again, "Tell me, what shall I give you?"

And Jacob said, "You shall not be giving me anything. For if you do this for me, I will again look after your flocks and they will increase for you. And you will be the one who gains. Let me pass through the sheep and goats, and let me take from them every mottled one; and they alone shall be my hire. And when you come to look over that which I have separated out, every one that is not mottled among the goats, and the sheep, that shall you count stolen."

And Laban said, "Would that it might be according to your word." And that day Laban removed all the goats and all the sheep that were mottled, and gave them into the hand of his sons, so that Jacob might not have them, and then rode away. And he set three days journey between him and Jacob.

But Jacob turned the pages of the Book that was long ago Adam and Eve's, and with the knowledge therein he took him rods of fresh poplar, and rods of the plane tree and the almond tree, and he peeled them a little till the white appeared and they were mottled. And he laid the mottled rods in the watering-troughs where the flocks came to drink. And when those sheep, and the goats, also had their young, they were born mottled. And he put those aside for himself.

And he continued to put the rods close to the flocks, but he chose only those that were strong. When the flocks that were weak came to drink, he put not the rods in. So the feebler flocks were for Laban, and the stronger for Jacob.

And this he did for six years more, with the help of the Book. And he increased his flocks exceedingly, so much that some he sold. And thus he had maid-servants and man-servants and camels and asses.

And Laban's sons said, "Jacob has taken away all that was our father's." And Jacob saw the face of Laban and it was not turned towards him.

And God said to Jacob, "Return now to the land of your fathers. I will be with you."

THE MEETING ON THE MOUNTAIN

And now, hundreds of years after the Garden of Delight, Jacob, who had come to Laban's house a poor man, babbling of Eliphaz, was rich. For he had built up for himself many herds of sheep and goats and servants. And he called to him Rachel and Leah, and said to them, "I see your father's countenance, that it is not turned towards me as before.

"Yet you know that with all my power I have served your father. And he has mocked me, and changed my wages many times. But the God of my father has been with me and suffered him not to hurt me. For if Laban said, 'The speckled shall be your wages', then all the flock bore speckled. If he said, 'The streaked shall be your wages', then all the flock bore streaked. Thus God hath taken away all the cattle of your father and given them to me. And now God has told me to return to the land of my Nativity."

And Rachel and Leah said, "What is there for us in our father's house? Did he not sell us to you so that you should work for him? Are we not accounted by him strangers?

"All the riches which God has taken away from our father and given to you, are ours and our children's. So whatever God has said to you, do, and we will go with you."

So Jacob set his wives and his children upon camels, and collected all his cattle, and all things which he had gathered together and loaded upon asses, and set forth for the home of Isaac his father in the land of Canaan.

Now at this time Laban was gone to shear his sheep, three days distance away. And Jacob outwitted Laban in that he told him not of his going. And Rachel stole the teraphim that were her father's, that had whispered to him about Jacob.

For she too wished to have their service. And she laughed to herself, "I have stolen Laban's heart"; for they were important to him. And they rode away.

Now when Laban returned to Padam-Aram, the shearing being over, he found the well was dry. So did he know at once that Jacob had gone. For since the moment Rachel and Jacob had met there and Jacob had rolled away the stone, the water had brimmed to the top, and over. So he pursued them for seven days.

But in a dream of the night God came to Laban and said, "Take good care that you speak to Jacob neither good nor bad." So it was that when Laban and Jacob met on the mountain, Laban remembered the dream of the night, and spoke carefully to Jacob. And he said, "What have you done, that you have carried away my daughters as though captives of the sword? Why did you outwit me, and flee secretly? Why did you not tell me, that I might have sent you away with merriment and mirth and music and celebration? And why did you not suffer me to kiss my daughters and grandchildren? This was not fitting of you!

"Did you not come to me in poverty and did I not feed you? Did I not give you my own kindred to make deeper the bond between us?

"Truly it is in the voice of my heart and the power of my hand to do you hurt. But the God of your father spoke to me in a dream of the night, saying, 'Take heed to yourself that you speak not to Jacob either good or bad.' So do I curb my words. And now that you have surely gone, because you long for your father's house, why have you stolen my gods?"

And Jacob said, "As for the first, I did not tell you because I was afraid you would hold your daughters from me. But as for the second, I have stolen nothing. Seek out whatever is yours with me, and whoever has taken your gods that person shall die." For he knew not that Rachel had taken them.

Then Laban went into Jacob's tent and into Leah's tent and into the tent of the two maidservants. And he searched, and found them not. Then went he into Rachel's tent.

Now Rachel had put the images in the saddle of the camel, and she sat upon them. And Laban felt all about the tent, and found them not. And Rachel said, "Let not my lord be angry that I cannot rise up before you. But today is the time of the month when the manner of women is upon me." So he touched her not, but continued to search, and he found not the teraphim.

Then Jacob raised his voice and said, "What is my trespass? What is my sin, that you hotly pursue me? What right have you to search through my belongings? What have you found that belongs to you? Set it down here between my people and your people that they may judge.

"Twenty years have I been with you! Your sheep and your goats have not lost their young, nor have I consumed any of them. That which was torn by wild beasts I did not bring to you, but I myself bore the loss of it, whether stolen by day or stolen by night; for that did you require of me! In the day the drought consumed me, and the frost by night, and my sleep fled from my eyes – thus I was!

"Twenty years have I been in your house, fourteen years for your two daughters, and six for your flock! And you have changed my wages many times! The God of my fathers has been on my side, or you would surely have sent me away with nothing! God has seen my misery and the labour of my hands, and gave judgement yesternight."

And Laban said mildly to Jacob, "The daughters are my daughters, and the children are my children, and the flocks are my flocks, and all that you see is mine. What more can I do this day? Come, let us make a covenant, you and I."

So Laban and Jacob made their covenant, and they ate bread together, and tarried together all night on the mountain. And in the morning, Laban kissed his daughters and his grandchildren and departed into his own place. And Jacob moved on. And he moved towards Esau.

CROSSING THE RIVER

Now Jacob turned towards home. For he remembered what God had said when, after betraying his father and robbing his brother, he had lain on the ground outside the city and dreamed a dream. And in this dream God had said, "Behold I am with you, and I will keep you wherever you go, and will bring you back into this land."

But his heart was faint within him, for he never ceased remembering what he had done to Esau.

And he stood on the bank of the river Jabbok, Esau being on the other side. And he sent messengers before him to Esau, and he commanded them, "Thus shall you say unto my lord Esau, 'Your servant Jacob speaks, saying, I have sojourned with Laban and stayed until now; I have oxen, and asses, and flocks, I have men-servants and I have maid-servants; and I have sent to tell my lord, so that I might find favour in your sight.'"

And the messengers returned to Jacob, saying, "We came to your brother Esau. And he comes with four hundred men."

Then Jacob was greatly afraid. And he divided the people that were with him, and the flocks and the herds and the camels, into two camps, for he said, "If Esau comes to the one camp and smites it, then the camp which is left shall escape." And Jacob said, "O God of my father Abraham, and God of my father Isaac, who didst say to me, 'Return to your country, and your family, and I will do you good', I am not worthy of the attention you pay me. You said to me, indeed you said, 'I will surely do you good, and make your children and your grandchildren as many as the grains of the sands of the sea, which cannot be counted for their multitude.' O deliver me, I pray you, from the hand of my brother, from the hand of Esau, for I fear him, lest he come and smite me, and the mothers and the children!"

And he thought what to do, and made from what he had a present for his brother Esau. Two hundred she-goats and twenty he-goats in one group, two hundred ewes and twenty rams in a second group, thirty milch camels and their colts in a third, forty kine and ten bulls in a fourth, and twenty she-asses and their foals in a fifth group, all gathered together from his own. And he gave each group to a servant to drive; and he said to the servants, "Pass over before me, each with your drove. And put a space between drove and drove."

And to the foremost he said, "When Esau my brother meets you, and asks you, 'Whose servant are you, and whither do you go, and whose are these before you?' you shall say 'Lord, they are your servant Jacob's. He sends them as a present to my lord, even my lord Esau. And behold he comes behind us.'" And he commanded the second servant, and the third, and all that followed the droves, saying, "In this manner shall you speak to Esau, always ending 'And your servant Jacob is behind us.'" For he thought, "I will soften his anger with these presents that go before me, and then as he comes towards me I will see his face, and know if perchance he will accept me."

So each group, turn by turn, with space in between, crossed the ford of the river. Yet Jacob still remained behind.

And that night he rose up, and he took Rachel and Leah and his two handmaids, and all eleven children, and sent them also over the ford of the rushing river. And after them he sent all else that he had. But he himself remained still behind. And now he was alone.

And that night a stranger came and fought with him, to force him over the river. But he would not go. They struggled together. And the stranger did wound him in the thigh; but he clung to him, and still they struggled together.

Then the stranger said, "Let go of me, for the day is breaking. And you must go to meet Esau, and I must go to praise God."

And Jacob said, "I will not let go, till you tell me I am safe."

And the stranger said, "I will tell you one thing only. You shall no more be called Jacob, which is 'cheat' and 'fraud', but Israel. For Israel means 'one who has struggled with God and with men, and become strong'. And he blessed him.

And Jacob at last passed over the river Jabbok, just as the sun rose.

And behold, now Esau was approaching, and with him four hundred men. And Jacob lifted up his eyes and saw him. And he divided the children unto Leah and unto Rachel, and unto the two handmaids. And he put the handmaids and their children foremost, and Leah and her children after, and Rachel and Joseph hindmost. And he himself passed over before them all. And he bowed himself down to the ground seven times for fear, until he came near to his brother.

Then Esau ran to meet him, and embraced him, and fell on his neck, and kissed him. And they wept - Esau for honest joy, Jacob for relief.

And Esau lifted up his eyes and saw the women and the

children, and said, "Who are all these with you, brother?"

And Jacob said, "God in mercy has given them to your slave."

And Esau said, "And what are yonder herds and drovers, brother?"

And Jacob said, "They are my gift to you."

Then Esau said, "No brother, no. I have enough. Let what you have stay yours."

But Jacob urged him, saying, "No, I pray you. If I have found favour in your sight, receive the present I give you. For I have seen your face, as I have seen the face of God, and it has love for me. Take my gift. Let it be a blessing for you. For God has dealt graciously with me, and I have enough." So Esau took them.

Then said Esau, "Come ride with me to my city. I will come beside you and we shall go together."

And Jacob said, "My lord, the children are tender, and the lambs and calves that still feed from their mothers are a care to me, and if we overdrive them only one day, they will all surely die. Let my lord, I pray you, go on before his servant Jacob. And I will journey on more gently, according to the pace of the children and the cattle, until we come to you."

And Esau said, "Let me at least leave with you some of those that are with me, that they may escort you and see you safe."

And Jacob said, "There is no need, I pray you."

So Esau returned to his home to prepare a banquet for Jacob and all his household. For did not his mother once say that his anger died away like a fire of thorns?

But Jacob did not follow him and banquet with him,

for he was not a man who had much trust in others. But he turned another way.

Now as they travelled on towards Canaan, and it was a long hard journey, Rachel gave birth to a child. And her time was full of pain. And the midwife said to her, "Fear not. See, it is another son for you." But the spirit was departing from Rachel, and she spoke softly to Jacob, and her voice was a flickering candleflame. And she said, "Call the child Ben-oni, for he will be a child of mourning, a child of grief."

And Jacob fell before her and cried, "No! Call him Benjamin, child of strength. You shall live!" And Jacob gave the child that name, for his fierce love of Rachel.

Yet still Rachel died. For had not Jacob said, when Laban searched the tent, "If any has stolen what is yours, let that one die"? And what is said cannot be unsaid, though it be said unknowingly. And Rachel was very lovely and beautiful to all living, and very dear to Jacob.

THE DREAMER

Now Jacob had the Cloak of Adam and Eve, and it still smelled of the apples and the spices of the Garden of Delight. And he had the Staff that was also a Sword, that was blue as the sapphire sky, and signed with God's name. And he had the Book of All Knowledge Worth Knowing, which was mysteries of past, present, and future, and warnings and healings. For he had stolen them all from his brother Esau, when his mother had said, "They should be yours."

And now that Jacob was an old man with many children, he thought he would one day give the Cloak and the Book and the Staff to his son Joseph. For he loved this one more than all his children, because he was the son of his old age, and because he was the child of Rachel when she was strong, and because, like Rachel, he was beguiling. For when Jacob saw the curl of his eyelash on his cheek, and the curl of his hair on his brow, like tiny sickle moons, he wept and said, "That is Rachel." And when he saw his scheming ways, he laughed and said, "That is Jacob."

So while the brothers followed the sheep in the fields and the hills of Canaan, he took the Book from its casket, and opened it, and together they studied its Mysteries – how to be learned in the speech of the thunderclaps, how to know the time of birth and the time of death, and how to do wondrous deeds. And to the boy the whole world seemed but an open book full of coloured pictures where he saw his own face.

And in Jacob's delight, he made Joseph an embroidered coat of many colours, with wide flowing sleeves, yet so lovely and delicate it could be crushed and concealed in the palm of a hand. And when Joseph raised his arm, the sun shone through it, as it were a rainbow. But his brothers could not speak peaceably to him.

And Joseph began to touch his eyes with paint, and cut his hair in the way of women, and put perfume on his ears, and sweet balm on his body, and gathered together garments of all textures and all colours, and wore them most gracefully. And he was beautiful as an olive tree, so that Jacob's heart ached, and he smiled on him.

And Joseph dreamed dreams, and told them to his brothers. Such as, "Behold, I dreamed we were binding sheaves in the field, and lo, my sheaf arose and stood upright, and your sheaves came round about, and bowed down to my sheaf." And they said, "Shall he indeed reign over us?" and mocked him.

And he dreamed another dream, and told them, saying, "Behold, I dreamed you were gathering fruit, and so did I. But yours rotted, whereas mine was sweet and juicy and plentiful."

And he dreamed yet another dream, and told it, this to his brothers and his father also, saying, "I saw the sun and the moon and eleven stars, and they bowed down to me."

And his father, even Jacob, rebuked him, saying, "What is this dream that you have dreamed! Shall I and your mother and your eleven brothers indeed come to bow down to you? Is not your mother dead? Let there be an end to this childish prattle." But he fondled him. And his brothers hated him yet the more for his dreams and his coat and his eyes and his words and his father's fondling.

Now it happened when Joseph was seventeen years of age, and his brothers that were sons of the handmaidens had taken the sheep to pasture, that Jacob sent him to help them in the fields. But the wind blew on him and ruffled his hair, and disturbed the folds of his coat of many colours, and made his eyes run so that the paint smarted and his eyes ran the more. And it was a hot wind, and a burning wind, so that insects fell like rain about him. And he liked not the smell of the sheep, nor of his brothers. So he returned. And wanting not to explain what had displeased him, he told Jacob that his brothers did many things that Jacob would not like, and that, for this, he could not stand to be with them.

When days had passed, Jacob sent him again to his brothers. And on the night of that day, when beasts of the dark came up from their holes or down from the trees, his brother Gad saw a branch move, and heard a twig snap, and he knew a wild beast was creeping stealthily on the lambs. Now Gad was a good and powerful shepherd, and when a lion approached the lambs, he would pursue it, grip it by the foot, fling it a stone's throw from him, and kill it thus. So did he that time; for a great bear crept on the fold and snatched a lamb. And Gad curled the fingers of his huge hand into the bear's flanks and hurled it against a rock, and battered it down with his club.

But the lamb was grievous hurt, and past saving, and Gad killed it too, to end its pain. And later the brothers took it, and cooked it, and ate it for their meal in the fields.

Then Joseph returned home, and told Jacob that his brothers chose the choicest rams of his flock, and killed them and banqueted on them. And whatever Joseph told him, he believed, and he reproached the brothers. And Gad swore he wished never to see Joseph again, else he would destroy him from off the land of the living.

Then did Jacob send him to his other brothers, the sons of Leah. But he returned from them also, saying they consorted with evil women of the land, and that they spoke of their brothers, the sons of the handmaids, Gad and the rest, as slaves, and that he was ashamed to be with them.

Then did Jacob keep Joseph with him and sent him to his brothers no more. And Joseph wrote his dreams in a book, recording the day and the hour and the place, and all that had happened round about. For God said to him, "Take heed. Only wait. These things that you dream will surely come to pass."

THE SALE

So Joseph in his coat of many colours dreamed dreams, and studied mysteries.

Now it happened one day that his brothers had led the flocks to the pastures of Shechem; and they had not returned. And Jacob said, "Perchance some evil has befallen them. Perchance some anger has sprung up between them and the people of the land."

And he sent Joseph to find them and bring him back word, whether they were safe or no.

So Joseph went out of the Vale of Hebron, and he came to Shechem. And a man found him wandering in the fields and said, "Seek you someone?"

And he said, "I seek my brethren. Tell me, I pray you, where they feed their flock."

And the man said, "They are gone from here. I heard them say, 'Let us move on to Dothan.'"

So Joseph went after his brethren, seeking them, not to return back till he had found them. And they saw him coming a long way off, in his coat of many colours, and they said one to another, "The dreamer comes!" And one said, "Let us set dogs on him"; and they laughed.

And before he came close to them, they conspired together and one said, "The master of dreams comes with a new dream. Let us kill him and cast him into a pit. And we will say an evil beast has devoured him. Then we shall see what becomes of his dreams!"

Then Reuben, the eldest of them, saw that they laughed no more, but were decided. And he said, "No, let us not take his life. Let us not shed his blood. Let us cast him into this pit that is in the wilderness, but lay no hand on him": for he meant to deliver the lad out of their hands and restore him to his father at a later time.

So it came to pass, when Joseph was come near to them, that the brothers seized him, and stripped him of his coat of many colours, and they cast him into the pit. And the pit was a dried well, having no water, only snakes and scorpions. And they left him there for three days and three nights; for they thought, he will die, and none shall find him; and we will not have killed him with our bare hands. And Reuben could not yet rescue him, for he had gone to do work in further fields.

Then did a caravan of merchantmen come by, loaded with skins of animals; and Joseph did still cry out. And the brothers said one to another, "They will take him on their journeyings. So will he disappear among the peoples of the earth." And they took Joseph roughly out of the pit, heeding not his cries, and sold him to the merchantmen.

And when Reuben returned from the work that was his, and let down a rope into the pit, Joseph was not there. And Reuben wept, for he was the oldest and would have to account to his father. And he returned to his brothers and said, "The child is not there! And as for me, where shall I hide myself!"

But they paid him no heed. And they took Joseph's coat of many colours which lay on the ground, and ripped it. And they killed a goat, and dipped the coat in the blood. And they brought it to their father and said, "This have we found. Know now whether it is Joseph's coat, or not."

And he looked and said, "It is his. It is Joseph's." And he said, "A wild beast has devoured him. He is without doubt torn in pieces." And he said, "I sent him to you to see if all was well with you and the flock"; and they said "He came not."

Then Jacob cried aloud. And he said, "Catch me the first wild beast you see, and deliver him to me for vengeance!" And they brought him a wolf. And he said to the wolf, "Murderous wretch! Do you respect neither God nor me!" And God granted the wolf human speech to answer (for in all the years since the Garden of Delight, beasts and humans had ceased to use the one language, and now each spoke his own tongue.)

And the wolf said, in the words of humans, "By the life of our Creator, I am innocent! Twelve days ago, my own son left me. I knew not if he were dead or alive, and I hurried to Dothan in search of him. Take what vengeance you please in your own anguish! But I swear to you, I have never set eyes on your son. Nor indeed has human flesh ever passed my lips."

Jacob marvelled, for it was long since beast and humankind had spoken one to another, and had spoken of the same sorrow. And he let the wolf go. And Jacob wept for Joseph many days. And all his sons and all his daughters-in-law rose up to comfort him; and he said, "Nay, I shall never be comforted. I will go down to the grave still mourning."

ZULEIKA

Now the merchantmen had bound Joseph on to the camel's back, so that his face was against the creature's rough hair, and it was sour smelling and full of fleas. And he said, "Pray untie me, and let me descend, and walk." For since the snakes and scorpions had not harmed him but had crept away from him into the cracks and crevices of the pit, being so commanded by God, he was only hungry and shaken. And the merchants did not understand the words, but they let him walk.

And seeing his astonishing beauty and the grace of his perfumed body, they began to say one to another, "Perchance they were robbers, for the boy seems of finer ilk than they. Perchance he is of noble family. Perchance even now his true kin follow us, and will kill us. For it must be the lad has been stolen." And when they came unto Egypt, they hastened to sell him in the market, that they might be rid of him and gone. And they sold him to Potiphar, an officer of Pharaoh's, the Governor of his Royal Prison, for some pieces of silver, and quickly went.

And Joseph pleased Potiphar. And within a small time, Potiphar said, "He is worthy of a prince's place," and made him close to one of his family. And he ordered him to be taught music, and drawing also, and many fine arts beside; and he gave him food of a most goodly kind, that far passed the food of other slaves. And he said, "The boy is an enchanter. If he brings to me spiced wine and I would fain have bitter wine, straightway is the spiced wine turned into bitter. I have but to wish."

And he made him overseer over all that he had, save his

wife, and gave him the keys of his house. For he saw God was with Joseph, and would make all that he did prosper. And Joseph began again to paint his eyes, and to curl his hair, and to walk elegantly. And his beauty was still as the olive-tree, and his scent was as the wine of Lebanon.

Now Potiphar had a wife, Zuleika, who was fair to look on, and he could not behave to her as a man should to his wife. So that Zuleika looked on Joseph, and sighed, and reached for his hand in secret. But Joseph said, "He has kept nothing from me but you, who are his wife. I will not do this thing."

And Zuleika said to him, "How beautiful is your hair. Take my golden comb, and comb it." But he would not. And she dressed in a new and astonishing garment each day; and she bedecked herself with jewels that deceived the eye, alternately blazing forth and fading. But he turned away his face. Then she put love potions in his food and drink, but God sent the angel Gabriel to change the cups, and move his hand from the dish.

Then she gave him silken garments, of one kind for the morning, of one kind for the noon, of a third kind for the evening. But he would not wear them.

Then she spoke to him in anger. "I shall order you beaten!"

"God helps those who are beaten," he answered.

"I shall starve you!"

"God feeds the hungry."

"I shall cast you into prison!"

"God releases the captive."

So she grew pale. And the ladies of the court said, "What ails you? Are you sick?"

And Zuleika said, "You shall see what ails me, and you shall tell me if I do not have good cause."

And she ordered a banquet, and she sent for Joseph to serve. And the ladies of the court came at her invitation. And when they peeled the fruit that was before them with their little knives, they could not forbear to watch Joseph, for he was so exquisite to look on; and they cut their hands one after another, and there was blood on the fruit.

And when Joseph left the hall, Zuleika said, "Your blood is on the fruit. If you cut your fingers after so little torment, how can I endure the full days?"

And she said, "I know it is told in the stars he will love a woman of Potiphar's household."

And they sighed and fluttered their eyelids, and advised her, saying, "You must be with him alone. Then he cannot resist you."

Then came the night when the Nile exceeds its banks and enriches the land, the Festival that is called even today 'The Night Isis Weeps'. And all were gone to the river, with harps and drums and with dancing. And Joseph remained in the house to do his work, and there was no man with him. (And this was the same house in which Pharaoh had tried to hold Sarai, when Abram hid her in a chest many many years past; and the house remembered and was waiting.)

And when all were gone to the river, and only the sound of the distant drums could be heard, Zuleika entered Joseph's room, and said to him, "My true love, now are we alone." And she tore off his garment.

And he turned to her, and would have embraced her, but that Jacob his father, who was in Canaan, rose up between them and shook his head; so that he retreated. And Zuleika cried out, "My friend, oh my true love, why so affrighted?"

And he said, "My father is here."

And she said, "There is no-one here. We are alone. The palace is empty."

And he said, "I belong to those who see things." Then he fled from her. And she cried with a loud shrill cry.

Then many servants came running, with spears. And she cried to them, "Take this slave! He has attacked me!" For she was both angry and sorrowful, and afraid of what might befall.

And she saw that his garment was in her hand, and she laid it by her till her lord came home. And she spoke to her lord thus-wise, saying, "The servant whom you have brought us came in unto me, to mock me. And I lifted up my voice, and cried out, and he fled. But I caught at his robe to show his wantonness."

And they took Joseph, and they set him before the judges, and showed them the piece of cloth. And the judges said, "If this piece of cloth be torn from the back of his garment, then was he truly running from her because she cried out against him; and she indeed tore his garment to have proof of his wantonness. But if it be torn from the front of his garment, then she tore it to arouse his passion." And they looked on it, and all said it was torn from the front.

Nevertheless they threw Joseph into prison. And he stayed there for ten years, and after that for two more. And those two were a time of waiting; for the memory of Pharaoh and the memory of the cupbearer were transfixed till the two years passed, as a stream is frozen till the spring comes. But that is a later story, and comes in its own time, and will be told.

THE TWO PRISONERS

So it had come to pass that Joseph's brothers, being angry that their father loved him more than they, and being angered also by his beauty and his dreams, had sold him into slavery in Egypt. (And for this, their children and their children's children, and the children of them also, would be slaves in Egypt for many years to come. But that is a later story, and they did not know it.) And now that Joseph was in prison, he spoke humbly and lowered his eyes, being a prisoner; but he well knew how languorously his lashes lay against his cheek. And he still had favour in the sight of Potiphar, who was Governor of the Royal Prison. And Potiphar committed to Joseph's hand all the prisoners that were in the prison, so that whatsoever they did there, Joseph had knowledge of.

Now it happened one day in the house of Pharaoh, great ruler of all Egypt, that when food was set on the Royal table, a fly was found in Pharaoh's wine cup, and a hard lump in his bread. And Pharaoh was wrath against the chief cupbearer and the chief baker that they should have offended him; and he cast them into prison, into the place where Joseph was bound.

And it came to pass that the baker and the cupbearer each dreamed a dream one night. And Joseph came in unto them in the morning, and they were troubled. And they said unto him, "We have dreamed a dream, and there is none that can interpret it."

And Joseph said, "Interpretations belong to God. Perhaps God will put it in my mouth. Tell it to me." So they told him each his dream.

And the chief cupbearer said to him, "Behold, a vine was before me, and in the vine were three branches. And as it was yet budding, immediately did blossoms shoot from it, and swiftly after clusters of ripe grapes. And Pharaoh's cup was in my hand. So I took the grapes and pressed them into Pharaoh's cup; and I gave the cup into Pharaoh's hand."

And Joseph said to him, "Thus says your dream. Within three days, Pharaoh shall lift up your head and restore you unto your office, and you shall give his cup into his hand, as of old." And he said also, "But remember me when it shall be well with you, and make mention of me unto Pharaoh, and bring me out of this house. For indeed I was stolen away from my home; and here also have I done nothing that they should put me into the dungeon. I pray, remember me."

When the chief baker saw that the interpretation was good, and that Joseph beseeched the cupbearer to speak to Pharaoh about him, being therefore sure what he said would come to pass, he said, "Speak to me also. In my dream, behold, three baskets were on my head; and in the uppermost basket were all manner of baked bread and cakes for Pharaoh. And the birds did fly down and eat them all."

And Joseph said, "This is the interpretation. Within three days, Pharaoh shall lift up your head from off you, and hang you on a tree. And the vultures shall come down and eat you."

And what he said of their dreams came to pass. For in three days was the birthday of Pharaoh. And he gave a feast for all his slaves. And he restored the chief cupbearer unto his office, so that he gave the cup again unto Pharaoh's hand. But the chief baker he hanged.

And yet the chief cupbearer did not remember Joseph as he had promised, but forgot him.

THE REVEALER OF SECRETS

Now ten years had passed since Joseph had been thrown
into prison because of the passion of Zuleika. And now the
baker and the cupbearer had each been dealt with according
to the command of Pharaoh, which was as God, speaking
through Joseph's mouth, had said it. And Joseph himself
should have been freed, for ten whole years had passed.
But Joseph had thought to charm the cupbearer as he had oft
charmed Jacob, asking him to bring him out of prison. And
God said, "He is still in love with his own beautiful eyes. He
has not yet faith in me. He shall stay two years more, and learn."

So the next two years were years of frozen time. Each
night Pharaoh dreamed. But each morning, when he woke,
he forgot his dream. For the time was not yet come. And
each night, the cupbearer tied a knot in his handkerchief,
that he might remember on the morrow to tell Pharaoh of
the beautiful youth who knew the language of dreams. But
every morning before he awoke the angel Michael untied
it, and he forgot. For the time was not yet come.

But after the two years had passed, Pharaoh awoke and
now he remembered he had dreamed. And now he
remembered what he saw in the dream. He stood by the river
Nile. And seven cows stepped out of the river, sleek and well-
favoured, and they grazed on the reeds. Then seven other cows
stepped out of the river; but they were lean and ill-favoured.
And they stood on the brink of the river, and they ate up the
seven cows that were fat and sleek. Then Pharaoh awoke.

And he slept and dreamed a second time. And behold
he saw seven ears of corn growing on one single stalk, fat
and good. And another stalk sprang up, with seven ears also,

but thin and blasted with the east wind. And the thin withered ears swallowed up the fat round ears. And Pharaoh awoke. And he remembered this dream also.

And it was morning, and his spirit was troubled, and circled over his dreams like birds over a dying man. But no-one could interpret.

Then he sent for others who came from afar, from Goshen and Mizraim, and Raamses and Zoan, and from all the cities of Egypt. But still none could interpret.

And Pharaoh grew angry, and the wise men grew fearful. And one said, "The seven sleek kine are a sign you will have seven beautiful daughters. The lean ones, that they will waste, and die." And another said, "The seven plump ears of corn are a sign that you will conquer seven nations. The withered ones that they will be no pleasure to you."

But when a dream is right interpreted, the dreamer knows, for a weight falls from him. And Pharaoh was still burdened, and he cried out, "Is there none that can tell me true?" And he ordered his executioner to take them one and all, and execute them.

At that moment, the chief cupbearer looked at his handkerchief, and there was a knot therein, and he remembered. And he said, "O mighty king, be not angry. Stay the hand of your executioner. For there is a slave in the Royal dungeon that will interpret your dream. Did not I and the chief baker dream a dream in the one night, each his own dream? And as he told us, so did it come to pass."

And Pharaoh said, "Bring him here!"

So they sent to the prison. And they shaved Joseph's face, and they cut his hair, and they bathed him, and put on him clean and wholesome garments, and they took him from the dungeon and brought him before Pharaoh.

And Pharaoh sat on the Royal throne of gold and silver, and his jewels flamed.

And he said to Joseph, "I have dreamed a dream, and there is none that can interpret it. And I have heard it said of you that you speak the language of dreams."

And Joseph said, "It is not I who speak it, but God who speaks through my mouth."

Then Pharaoh said, "In my dream, behold, I stood upon the brink of the river. And seven kine came out of the water, sleek and well-favoured, and they fed in the reed-grass. And seven other kine came after them, poor and thin and ill favoured, such as I have never seen in all the land of Egypt for badness. And the lean and ill-favoured did eat up the fat and sleek ones. And when they had eaten them, it could not be known they had eaten them, for they were as thin as at the beginning. And I awoke.

"But I fell asleep and dreamed again. And I saw in my dream, seven ears of corn come up on one stalk, full and fat. And seven further ears of corn, withered, thin, and blasted by the east wind, sprang up after them. And the withered ears swallowed up the seven good ears.

"And I told all this to my magicians. But there was none that could declare it unto me."

And Joseph said to Pharaoh, "The two dreams are one. The seven good kine are seven good years. The seven good ears are seven good years. And the seven lean kine and the seven empty ears are seven years of famine. The dream is one.

"There shall come seven years of great plenty throughout all the land of Egypt. And after there shall be seven years of famine. And the famine shall be so grievous, that it shall swallow up the plenty, and it will be as if the plenty had never been.

"God sends dreams not to grieve us, nor to frighten us, but that we might understand the message, and act accordingly. What God is about to do has been shown unto Pharaoh. And since God will do it soon, it is shown twice in one night, that you may act swiftly.

"Therefore let Pharaoh look out a man who is discreet and wise, and set him over the land of Egypt. And let that man appoint overseers in these seven years of plenty, that corn from a fifth part of all the land of Egypt will be stored under the hand of Pharaoh against the seven years of famine which are to come; and the land perish not." And he spoke not further, but in his heart he exulted, and said "This is I."

And Pharaoh said to his astrologers, "Can we find another such as this?" And he said to Joseph, "There is none as discreet and wise as you, for in you is the spirit of God. According to your word shall my people be ruled, and without you none shall lift up hand or foot in the whole of Egypt. And only in the throne shall I, Pharaoh, be greater."

And Pharaoh took his signet ring from off his hand, and put it on the hand of Joseph. And he arrayed him in fine linen, and put a chain of gold about his neck, and a gold crown on his head, and set him in his second chariot which rode by the side of Pharaoh's own.

And Joseph rode through the land of Egypt. And thousands marched alongside him, some with cymbals, some with flutes, some with drawn swords; and one in front shouted "All bend the knee!" And women and maidens leaned from the windows, and threw down jewels and bracelets.

And Joseph was known to them ever after as 'The Revealer of Secrets'.

CORN IN EGYPT

So it came to pass, as Joseph had foretold, that there were seven years of plenty. And in those seven years he laid up corn as the sands of the sea. And then came the seven years of famine.

Now in the days when Joseph angered his brothers with his painted eyes, and his coloured coat and his dreams, he had studied the Book of All Knowledge with Jacob his father. And the corn that he stored away in Egypt lay in the embrace of its own soil, the dust that belonged to each separate field; for he knew from the Book that such was its need; and his corn was sweet and good. But the corn that the Egyptians had laid by was rotten and full of worms, for they knew this not.

So the people of Egypt cried to Pharaoh, "We have laid by the corn for seven years, and it is rotten. What now shall we do for bread?"

And Pharaoh said, "Go unto Joseph. What he says to you, do."

And Joseph opened all the Royal storehouses and sold to the Egyptians, and he took their money for Pharaoh. Then he took their cattle for Pharaoh. Then he took their land. Then he took themselves, their very bodies; and they became slaves to Pharaoh, for the sake of the corn. And with the corn they lived, and their families lived, and did not die.

And many countries also came into Egypt, to Joseph, and asked for corn. And they also gave their money to Pharaoh, through Joseph. For the famine was over the whole face of the earth. And the people had bread, and Pharaoh became most powerful, having many slaves because of Joseph. (And for this slavery of others, the family of Jacob and Joseph would pay, and for four hundred years they would be slaves themselves, till the Red Sea opened for them. But that is a later story.)

Now it came to Jacob's ears that there was corn in Egypt. And he said to his sons, "Why do you look one upon the other? Is it not time to go? There is corn in Egypt! Get you down thither, that we may live and not die."

And he said to them, "Do not speak to anyone. Beware of jealous eyes. Enter the city each by a different gate. Never be seen speaking to each other. Be as shadows." For he was a man who did not trust others.

But Benjamin, Joseph's own brother, sent he not with them, for he also was the child of Rachel, and for him Rachel had died. And he said, "Peradventure some harm may befall him", and he kept him.

Now Joseph had commanded that each man who came for corn must write down his name, and his father's name, and his grandfather's; that it might be known who had come day by day. So he waited for his brothers, for he knew they need must come; for the famine was sore over the earth.

And it came to pass that he saw their names on that day's list. And he commanded his officers to seek them. And they found them in an evil quarter of the city. And they arrested them, and brought them to him. And the brothers bowed down before him, with their faces pressed to the earth.

And Joseph remembered his dream. And in the dream there were all eleven brothers; and here there were only ten. So he spoke to them harshly, having an interpreter present, as one who was Egyptian and knew not their language.

And he said, "Whence came you?"

And they answered humbly, "From the land of Canaan."

And he said, "What is your business?"

"To buy food."

"Why then did you enter this city each by a different gate?"

"So said our father to us...."

"Why were you in the evil quarter of the city?"

"We were there because we sought someone."

"Many go there to seek someone." And he wrinkled his nose. "Did you seek man or woman?"

And they wished to say that they had begun to think of their brother Joseph, whom years ago they had thrown into a pit, and had watched being tied to a camel bound for Egypt, and now they thought that so beautiful a boy might well have been sold for evil purposes in the dark quarter of the city; but they did not dare to speak of their doing, so they said, "We went to inquire about some lost goods."

"You are spies! You come from the enemies of Pharaoh, to report to them what you learn, that they may attack us in a weak place. Do I not see in my silver cup that reveals secrets that you sold a near kinsman to travelling merchants! You are bandits, and spies!"

And they said, afraid, "My lord, my lord, we, your servants, are twelve brothers, the sons of one man in the land of Canaan. And the youngest is this day with his father. And the other is dead."

Then Joseph said, "By Pharaoh's life, I shall see this youngest brother that you speak of, or I shall know you for liars also! One of you shall fetch him, while I imprison the rest!"

Then he enclosed them all in a dungeon, not even freeing the one. For he meant to confuse them with his waywardness. And they were most afraid. But on the third day of their imprisonment, he said to them, "I follow a merciful God. And this God tells me to keep only one of you hostage. The rest may return home, bearing the corn. But you shall bring back your youngest brother that I may see him, before this one is freed. Then I shall know you are honest men, and you shall all be free and not die."

And they said one to another, not knowing he understood their language, "This is because we abandoned Joseph. This is because we would not hear his cries, when he besought us."

And Reuben said, "Did I not say do not sin against the child!" For they thought the evil they did had turned against them. And they knew not that Joseph understood them, for the interpreter was between them. And Joseph turned from them and went into another room and wept.

When he returned to them, he chose Simeon from among them as his prisoner. And Simeon raged against his brothers. "Was it not enough for you what you did to Joseph? Do you intend to do it to me also?"

And he raged also against the Egyptians, saying, "There is no man alive who can put me in prison!" So that Manasseh, one of Joseph's two sons, rose up, dealt him one blow in the back of his neck, and chained him. And it is said Simeon said in amazement, "Surely that blow was dealt me by one of our house!" And they left him in chains, bewildered.

Then Joseph in secret commanded his servants to give them much provision for the journey, and to fill their sacks to the utmost; and he told them to restore every man's money into the sack.

And when they reached a lodging-house, and one of them opened his sack to give his ass provender, he espied his money. And their hearts failed them, and they turned trembling one to another, saying, "What is this that God has done to us? Will the Egyptian send soldiers after us, saying we are thieves?"

And they came to Jacob in the land of Canaan, and told him all that had befallen them. And they said, "The man, the lord of the land, spoke roughly to us, and took us for spies. And we said, 'We are upright men. We are not spies. We are twelve brothers. The youngest is this day with our father in the land of Canaan; and one is no longer with us.'

"And the man, the lord of the land, said, 'Hereby shall I know you are upright men. Leave one of your brothers with me, and take corn, and go your way. And bring back your youngest brother to me. Then shall I know you are not spies, and speak true. And I will deliver you all.'"

And it came to pass, as they finished speaking, and emptied their sacks before Jacob, that every single man's bundle of money was in his sack. And when they saw it, they were all afraid.

And Jacob said to them, "Me have you bereaved of my children! Joseph is not, Simeon is not, and now you will take Benjamin away!"

And Reuben said to him, "Deliver Benjamin into my hand, and I swear I will bring him back to you. If I do not, you shall slay my own two sons."

And Jacob said, "Benjamin shall not go down with you! For his brother is dead, and he only is left of the children of

Rachel. If harm were to befall him by the way in which you go, you would bring down my grey hairs in sorrow to the grave." And he would not speak to them, and he wept.

And it came to pass, they had eaten up the corn which they had brought out of Egypt, and famine was still sore in the land.

And Jacob said, "Go again, buy us a little food." And Judah said, "The man did earnestly forewarn us, saying, 'You shall not see my face except your youngest brother be with you.'"

And he said again to Jacob, "If you will send our brother with us, we will go. But if you do not send him, we will not go down.

"For thus the man said to us."

And Jacob said, "Why did you destroy me by telling the man you had another brother!"

And they said, "The man asked concerning us. He said, 'Is your father yet alive? Have you another brother also?' And we answered him according to his questions. Could we know he would say, 'Bring your brother down'?"

And Judah said, "Send the lad with me, and we will arise and go, that we may all live and not die – we, you, and all our little ones. I myself will be surety for him. If I bring him not back to you, may I be cursed and blamed for ever. Except we had lingered, we would surely have already returned a second time."

And their father said to them, "If it must be so, do what I say. Take of the choice fruits of the land, and carry down the mana present – a little balm, some spicery and laudanum, the best honey hard as stone, and nuts and almonds, and Tyrian snails to stain his garments purple. And take double money in your hand. And the money that was returned to you in the mouths of your sacks, take that also; perchance it was an oversight. And take Benjamin."

And he said, "O God, when you made heaven and earth, and they wished to stretch out further and further, you said 'Enough!' Say now 'Enough!' to my sorrows."

And they took the present, and they took double money, and they took Benjamin; and they went down to Egypt, and stood before Joseph.

And when Joseph saw Benjamin with them, he said to the steward of his house, "Bring the men into the house, and kill the beasts, and prepare the meat; for these men shall dine with me at noon."

The Song

And the men were afraid, being brought into Joseph's house. And they said, "It is because of the money that was put into our sacks. He means to take us for slaves."

And they spoke to the steward of the house, saying, "O my lord, we opened each man his sack, and in the mouth of each sack was our money, returned. And we have brought it back in our hand."

And they said again, "We have brought other money with us to buy corn. We know not who put the first money back in our sacks."

And the steward said, "Peace be to you. Fear not. It was your God who is the God of your father who put treasure in the sacks for you. I already had your money."

And he brought Simeon out to them. And he brought them all into Joseph's house, and they washed their feet, and he gave their asses provender; and they made ready the present against Joseph's coming. And when Joseph came into the house, they brought it to him, and bowed down to the ground.

And he asked them of their welfare, and said, "Is your father well, the old man of whom you spoke? Is he yet alive?"

And they said, "He is well. He is yet alive." And they bowed their heads.

Then Joseph lifted up his eyes and saw Benjamin his brother, his mother's son, and he said, "Is this your youngest brother of whom you spoke to me? God be gracious to you, my friend."

And he made haste and went from the room, for his heart yearned towards his brother, and he sought where to weep. And he entered his own chamber and stayed there a while, then washed his face and came back.

And he restrained himself, and said, "Bring bread." And they brought bread for him, that ate by himself, and for the Egyptians, that ate at their own tables, and for the brothers, that ate at a table by themselves; for the brothers were of a race apart, and also they were shepherds, and for these two reasons no Egyptian would think to eat with them.

And Joseph had all the brothers seated in order of their age, with Reuben at the top, and descending by age. And the brothers marvelled at it, that he should know. And when it was Benjamin's turn to sit, Joseph said, "I know that the youngest among you has no brother of his own mother, near whom he can be seated. I neither. Let us therefore sit together, for we are of a kind." And they marvelled still more.

And he sent choice morsels of food from his own dishes to their table. And he took from his own plate and gave it to Benjamin. And when those around him saw what he did, they did likewise, to honour them. And the table of the brothers was heaped with delicacies, and Benjamin's plate was piled five times as high as the rest. And they drank from Joseph's goblets, and were merry with him.

And at daybreak Joseph spoke to the steward of his house, saying, "Fill the men's sacks with food, as much as they can carry. And put every man's money in the mouth of the sack. And in Benjamin's sack, put also my goblet, my silver goblet that reveals secrets." And so it was done.

And when the morning was light, and the men and their asses were out of the city but not yet far off, then Joseph said to his steward, "Up and follow them! And when you overtake them, say to them, 'Why have you stolen my lord's goblet, wherein he sees secrets? Is this not evil you have returned for good?'"

And he did so. And when he overtook the brothers, and said as Joseph had ordered him, they said, "My lord, why do you speak such words as these? Behold, the money which we found in our sacks' mouths we brought back to thee out of the land of Canaan. How then should we steal out of thy lord's house silver and gold?"

"You have it," he said.

And they said, "If it be in any man's sack, let that one die. And we also will be my lord's slaves."

And the steward answered, "You have spoken fairly. Yet my lord is merciful. Only he who has the cup shall suffer. He shall be made a slave. The rest are blameless."

Then they hastened, and took down every man his sack. And each opened his own. And the steward searched, beginning at the eldest.

And every man's money was in the mouth of the sack; and each was afraid.

But in Benjamin's sack was the goblet.

Then they cried aloud. And they loaded their asses, and returned to the city, and to Joseph's house, and fell on their knees before him. And Joseph said, "What madness was it? Did you think to prevent me revealing secrets?"

And Judah said, "What shall we say, my lord? How can we clear ourselves? We are innocent today, though long ago we were guilty, but of another charge. We are my lord's slaves, both we and the one who had the cup."

And Joseph answered, "No. Far be it from me to do so. The man with the cup shall be my slave. The rest, go in peace, unto your father."

Then Judah cried out, "What shall we tell him?"

And Joseph said, "Tell him that the rope has followed the bucket into the well." For he meant that the present follows the past, and all that happened now only followed what they had once done to him.

Then Judah came near to him and said, "O my lord, let your servant speak in your ears, and let not your anger burn against him; for you are as great as Pharaoh.

"My lord asked us, 'Have you a father, or a brother?' And we said, 'We have a father, an old man, and a child of his old age, a young one; and his brother is dead, and he alone is left of his mother, and his father loves him.' And you said to us, 'Bring him down to me.' And we said, 'The lad cannot leave his father; for if he did so, his father would die.' And you said, 'Except your youngest brother come with you, you shall see my face no more.'

"And it came to pass, when we came back to your servant, our father, we told him the words of our lord. And our father said, 'Rachel bore me two sons. And one went out from me, and I have not seen him again. And if you take this one from me, and harm befall him, you will bring down my grey hairs in sorrow to the grave.'

"So let me stay here, I pray you, instead of the lad, and let me be my lord's slave. For how shall I go to my father if the lad be not with me? How shall I look on the evil that shall come upon my father? Seeing his soul is bound up with the lad's soul, he will die."

Then Joseph could no longer hide himself. And he cried out, "Let every man go out from me, save these!" And when there stood no man with him save his brothers, he said to them, "I am Joseph."

And he wept aloud; and all the Egyptians heard his crying, and the house of Pharaoh heard.

And he said, shaking his head in wonder, "Is my father truly alive? Is he alive?" And they could not answer, for they were filled with fear and amazement.

And Joseph said to his brothers, "Come near to me, come near". And slowly they came near. And he said, "I am Joseph your brother, whom you sold unto Egypt. Be not grieved, or angry with yourself, that you did so, for I was sent before you that I might keep you alive when the time came.

"Go back to my father and say to him, 'Thus says your son Joseph: God has made me companion to Pharaoh and lord of all Egypt. Come down unto me. Tarry not. You shall dwell in the land of Goshen, and you shall be near to me, you, and your children, and your children's children, and your flocks and herds, and all that you have; and you shall not want.'"

And he said to his brothers, "Do not you see, do not the eyes of my own brother Benjamin see, that it is truly my mouth that speaks unto you, the mouth of Joseph? Tell my father of my glory in Egypt, and hasten!" And he kissed Benjamin, and he wept with him. And he kissed all his brothers. And then they wept, and talked together of many things.

And throughout Pharaoh's house, it was said, "Joseph's brothers are come."

And Pharaoh rejoiced for him, and said to him, "Say to your brothers thus: 'Take you chariots out of the land of Egypt for your wives and your little ones, and bring your father, and come. And do not squander time collecting your goods, for all the good things of the land of Egypt are yours.'"

And at Pharaoh's command, Joseph ordered raiment of gold and silver for them, and gifts for their families of ointments and spices, and coloured silks, and all sorts of precious stones, and many chariots to bring them back. And he sent twenty asses for Jacob, all laden with rich food and silver and gold ornaments, and with them a head-dress fit for an emperor. And he gave them many baskets of food for the journey. But to Benjamin he gave many times the rest, and because of this he said to them, "Do not fall out on the way", and they shook their heads, and tried to smile.

Now as they drew near to the house of Jacob, they hesitated. For he was an old man and full of days, and grey and bowed with grieving. And they said one to another, "How shall we tell him? Will he not die?"

And as they wondered and talked among themselves, a little child came dancing and singing among them, Serah, the great grandchild of Shem. God had given her beauty, wisdom and sagacity; and she was a singer and a musician, making up songs of all that was around her, and singing them for her own contentment. And she was three years old.

And they said to her, "Go to Jacob and sing to him." And she said, "What shall I sing?"

"Sing that Joseph lives," they said, "that he is in the land of Egypt." So the child Serah began to sing.

Joseph lives – O!
Joseph lives – O!
Yes he lives, yes he lives,

He lives, and loves, and laughs,
And he dances like Serah,
All in the land of Egypt - O!
Alleluya, God be praised,
Joseph lives - O!

And the music was sweet and artless as a bird in the morning. And as she sang, she danced, nearer and nearer to Jacob's house. And the brothers kept two full bow-shots behind.

Now Jacob was sitting outside, his head bowed and his eyes closed. And his thoughts were the thoughts of an old man, thoughts of his brother Esau from whom he had taken the Cloak of Adam and Eve to disguise himself, of his father Isaac whom he had deceived, of his mother Rebekah who protected him, of his wife Rachel for whom he had moved the stone in an instant from the well, and of his son Joseph with whom he had read over and over the Book of All Knowledge that is Worthy to be Known. And the dreams that Joseph once had, drifted in his mind like mist in the valley.

Then came Serah the little one, dancing round him singing.

Joseph lives - O!
Joseph lives - O!
Yes he lives, yes he lives,
He lives, and loves, and laughs,
And he dances like Serah
All in the land of Egypt - O!
Alleluya, God be praised,
Joseph lives - O!

He did not hear, being old, nor raised his head. But she heeded not, for being a child she danced and sang for her own delight.

> Joseph lives – O!
> Joseph lives – O!

And her voice soaked into his sorrow like rain into the parched ground. And at last he raised his head, and opened his eyes, and said, "Little one, that song again." And she sang again. "It is sweet to my ears," he said. And she sang again, dancing. "Come," he said. And she stopped her dance, and sat beside him, still singing. And in a little while the brothers came, and told him.

THE GOOD DAYS

Then Jacob laughed and cried for joy. And he made a banquet, and put on the royal robes and the royal head-dress that Joseph had sent him. And he bade all the kings around him to come and feast; and for three whole days and nights they ate and drank and sang together.

Then Jacob and his wives and his children and his children's children, even the littlest ones, gathered their horses and their asses, and their cattle and their sheep. And Jacob took up the Book of All Knowledge Worth Knowing, for he would once again read it with Joseph, and the sapphire Staff like the sapphire sky, and the Cloak of Adam and Eve that smelled of the Garden of Delight. And like a joyous stream that bubbles into sunlight, the people made their way through the hills and the valleys. For Joseph had said, "Come, I will look after you." And Pharaoh had said, "Do not linger. All the good things of Egypt are yours."

Sixty-nine people were with Jacob. And it is said in song and story that, as they reached the city wall, the sixty-nine became seventy, and there a child was born whom they named Jochabed. (But hers is a later story.)

And Joseph came out to meet them in his chariot of gold, that was second only to Pharaoh's. And with him came myriads of princes and astrologers and courtiers and nobles, dressed all in royal purple, and decked with jewels. And all moved to the rhythm of musical instruments of diverse kinds. And on the roof women clashed clanging cymbals and sang with joy of the coming of Jacob. For he was father of the great Revealer of Secrets, saviour of Egypt, and they honoured him.

And as Joseph drew near his father, he got down from

his chariot and ran to meet him. And seeing this, the princes and the nobles and the astrologers and the courtiers did likewise, all running towards Jacob, behind him.

And Jacob leaned on the sapphire Staff, blue as the sapphire sky and signed with God's name. And he got down from his chariot, and he also tried to run towards his son.

And Joseph bowed low before him, touching the ground. And the princes and the nobles and the astrologers and the courtiers did so also.

So it came to pass that in peace and prosperity and the sweet reflection of Joseph, Jacob and his wives and all his children and his children's children tended their flocks in the land of Goshen, which is in Egypt. And for all that they were shepherds, and strangers, and of another race, yet still the Egyptians revered them and praised them, for the sake of Joseph.

And the fish leapt out of the river and into their pots, and the grapes hung down in heavy tassels. So that they thought, "This is surely the land of milk and honey that God promised us. We thought it was Canaan, but it was Egypt."

And none thought then that there would arise a king in Egypt that knew not Joseph... who would be a hawk that casts its hovering shadow over the playful lambs, so that they are seized with fear and their heart stops. (But that is yet to come.)

Now it is said in song and story that there was a High Priest of Egypt whose name was Potiphera. He had a daughter. And she was as beautiful as Rebekah, as slender as Sarah, and as radiant as Rachel. Her name was Asenath.

She had many suitors, but would take none of them. Even the son of Pharaoh implored her many times, sending gifts of blazing jewels. But she sent them back, and said,

"My life is mine."

And she had seven maidens, whom she kept with her, who had all been born on the self-same day as she herself, and they lived together in her palace in loving and laughing sisterhood, and scorned all men.

Now it happened that Joseph wished to visit Potiphera, and he sent messengers to prepare the way. And Potiphera was pleased, and he made plans in his heart to marry Asenath to him.

But Asenath laughed, and her laughter licked round her father like a tongue of flame round a dry tree. "Shall I marry a slave!" she said. "One who was a shepherd, smelling of sheep and goats! I had sooner marry the son of Pharaoh – and him have I refused thirteen times!" And she was as passionate and proud as Lilith of the long loose hair who had left Adam and mocked the angels. And she would not agree to speak with him or to look at him. And her father could do naught with her.

But Joseph came to visit her father, in his chariot of gold, drawn by four snow-white horses. And Asenath saw him as she stood by the window of her palace, laughing with her maidens, and she knew not who he was; and she was suddenly silent. And she said slowly, "That man would I marry. I would be his for ever." And she did not cease looking, but said slowly again, "Who is that man?" And her seven maidens looked out of the window also, and sighed.

Yet was it not foretold they would marry? Had not Zuleika said to the ladies of the court when they cut their fingers at sight of Joseph, "He will love one of Potiphar's household, for the stars have said it"? But she had mistaken the name, for she was too eager. The stars had said Potiphera, and the stars were right, and the woman was Asenath, not Zuleika. And so it came to pass. And all the princes of Egypt came to the wedding feast, and for seven whole days wine glowed in goblets round as moons, and the wheat was ringed with flowers.

Now it happened that Jacob had said to God, being one who liked to have information that he might lay plans, "Would it not be well, oh Lord, that a man knew when he was going to die? – that a man fell ill, before he died? Then might he have time to get his house in order." (For until that time all had fallen down dead without warning.)

And God said, "Yes, that is so. You shall be the first."

So it was that when Jacob was one hundred and fifty-seven years old, he became ill. And he was the first one ever to do so, so that none knew why he did not rise, nor what to do. But Asenath, his daughter-in-law, understood; and she tended him.

And as he lay dying he asked for his Staff, and his Cloak, and his Book, that had once belonged to so many others – Adam and Eve, Seth, Methuselah, Noah, Shem, Abraham, Isaac and Esau his own brother and he gave them all to Joseph, for he had ever been his dearly beloved.

And Jacob died. And Pharaoh died, and his son also. And Joseph died, saying, "When you go to the land of milk and honey, take there my bones and bury them." And his brothers promised; but the land of milk and honey faded from their minds.

And the Cloak and the Book and the sapphire Staff vanished, and none knew where they were. And the eyes and the ears of the family of Jacob closed, and God spoke no more to them, not for many years. And they were still in Egypt when there arose a new king, who knew not Joseph, and remembered nothing.

THE JOYOUS TREE

And now there was a new king on the throne of Egypt, whose jewels flamed like the sun that sets the Nile ablaze. And he knew not Joseph who had been Revealer of Secrets and had worn the ring of Pharaoh. And the new king thought what to do with his new power.

"These people who throng our streets... speaking an outlandish tongue that is not ours... these strangers... what of them?" he said to his three counsellors.

"Mighty King," said Balaam, son of Peor, "these you speak of, they were seventy when they came, and now they are half a million."

"The air is full of turmoil and noise and change wherever they go," said Pharaoh.

"And, great lord," said Balaam, "they were once shepherds, who are vile to us!"

"Yet they are strong," said Pharaoh, musing.

"They are *even greater than we*," said Balaam.

"Did you say 'greater than we'?" said Pharaoh.

"Mighty King, did not lately our enemies invade us? And would have crushed us, being as many as the sands of the sea? But a mere handful of these strangers drove them out, with not one loss among them."

"They drove out our enemies," said Pharaoh, cautiously.

"They drive out our enemies today, O mighty King. But tomorrow? Who will they drive out tomorrow?"

"You speak well," said Pharaoh, and smiled.

"Advise us then what we should do," said Balaam.

"You are the advisor," said Pharaoh. "Speak."

Then Balaam said, "Mighty King, be cunning. Proclaim

that every citizen must make bricks and strengthen our fortifications that Egypt may be strong and defeat her enemies; and for this, each citizen will be well paid. And all will come.

"Then month by month, and secretly at first, we will send away our own people, till only the family of Jacob and Joseph is working, alone. And then we will increase their work till it be very grievous. And then, when they are completely in our hands, we will cease to pay them wages."

"And then?" said Pharaoh.

"Then they will die," said Balaam, and smiled. And Pharaoh thought, then smiled also.

"What think you?" he said to Ruel-called-Jethro, his second counsellor. And Ruel-called-Jethro said, "O King, live for ever. Four hundred years ago your grandfather called them here, for their prince Joseph had saved all Egypt from death. And your grandfather said to them, 'All the good things of the land of Egypt shall be yours.'"

And Pharaoh was angry and he said to Job, his third counsellor, "What say you?" But Job looked at his fingernails and said nothing.

Then Pharaoh did as Balaam had spoken. And by cunning the great family of Jacob and Joseph were made to build the fortifications without wages, and they cried aloud, and many died. Yet still their number increased.

Then Pharaoh sent again for his counsellors, Balaam, Ruel-called-Jethro, and Job. And Balaam said, "O mighty King, take their fields and their vineyards, take their cattle, take their food."

And Ruel-called-Jethro said, "O mighty King, their God is with them. Take care!" And Job looked at his fingernails, and said nothing.

Then Pharaoh did as Balaam said. And many of the children of Jacob and Joseph died. But still their number grew.

And Pharaoh called them again, Balaam, Ruel-called-Jethro, and Job. And at Balaam's counsel, he ordered them to work in the deep thick mud, to tread it with their bare feet, to mix it with straw to make bricks, that they must then bake in the glaring sun. And many died. And if those that continued to live did not make as many bricks as were demanded he had them beaten; and many more died.

Yet still there were new children born.

Then again at Balaam's counsel, he had them harnessed together like oxen, and he forced them to haul huge stones as big as cliffs that border the sea, to build walls for his cities; and he forced them to build their own children and their own comrades into the walls alive. And many died. And Pharaoh rejoiced at last - till he saw that the number of them grew no smaller, for still new children were born.

Then at Balaam's counsel, he called the midwives, who helped the mothers when their children were being born. And he said to them, "Every new-born boy you shall kill at his very first breath, that he may not become a warrior against us. But any girl you may leave alive and we will do with her what we wish, later on."

But the midwives did not do as Pharaoh commanded. And Pharaoh sent for them. And he said, "Why have you not obeyed me!"

And they said cunningly, "It is not our fault. The mothers are so strong and so full of life, their children are born before we come, and we do not even see them to do to them as you ordered."

Then one night Pharaoh dreamed a dream. And in his dream he saw a hand. And the hand between finger and thumb held a pair of scales. One pan of the scales was huge and made of gold, and jewelled kings and queens and warriors were crowded into it, and chariots and horses, and pyramids and granaries and palaces. And the other was tiny and sparse and made of sticks and straw like a sparrow's nest; and inside was nothing but one new-born baby.

And as he watched in his dream, that small straw pan, with naught but a baby inside, was so inexplicably powerful that it came down, down, forcing the gold pan up in the air. And the gold pan hung there, the palaces swaying and tottering, the kings and queens stumbling and screaming, till they all crashed down, and the buildings were smashed to dust.

And Pharaoh started out of his sleep with wild eyes, and he summoned his counsellors. And Balaam said, "O mighty King, write down the name of every woman, who is with child. And have your servants record these days as they pass. And when eight months have passed, put two guards in front of every house to wait for each child to be born. And if it is a son, have them cast it straightway into the river. For the stars have told that the child who menaces us is doomed to die by water." And Job looked at his fingernails, and said nothing. Till Pharaoh said, "Speak!"

And Job said, "O King, they are in your hands. Do to them what you will." (And for this, and for all his silences, he later suffered many plagues and sorrows, so that those who do not know his past have sighed for him. But that is another story for other books.)

Then Pharaoh said to Ruel-called-Jethro, "What say you?"

And Ruel-called-Jethro said, "O King, only cease to harm this people!" And Pharaoh was wild with rage and drove him out of his presence, so that Ruel-called-Jethro fled from Pharaoh's sight, and back to Midian where he was born.

But as he was about to flee, he remembered. And because he remembered, a sea would one day part its waters, and slaves and their children and a mixed multitude besides, two million in all with their flocks and herds, would pass through the sea, the waters reared up on either side of them. (But that is told in many a song and story, and will come in its time. Enough now to say, he remembered.)

He remembered that when Joseph died, certain Egyptians had broken into the dwelling that was Joseph's and pillaged it. Who they were is nowhere recorded, nor why they did it. But they had stolen from there the Three Gifts that once God had given to Adam and Eve when they left the Garden of Delight - the Cloak that would balance their coldness, the Book which would tell them the language of beasts and birds and even the thoughts of the rain, and the gentle Staff that could also be a sword. And the robbers had taken them to the Palace of Pharaoh; and there they had remained ever since. And none used them, or paid attention to them; and they were forgotten, as the nuts a squirrel hides when the leaves fall.

But Jethro remembered. And he sought them out. And he took them with him secretly back to Midian, the land of his birth.

But in his Palace, Pharaoh cared not that Jethro was

gone nor knew what he had taken, but did as Balaam counselled, and put guards in front of the houses, to record the days as they passed.

And women crept into the fields by night to give birth to their children secretly. And it is said in song and story they were born with long hair down to their knees to serve as a warm blanket, so that they lived. And the people of Jacob and Joseph wept, and cursed Pharaoh.

But Jethro walked in his garden in Midian. And he leaned on the Staff that he had brought with him. And it straightway stretched into the ground. And it grew roots, and leaves rushed out, and fruit burst upon the branches in scented glory. And in one minute it was a joyous tree. And it waited.

THE GIFT OF THE NILE

Now in those days time and space stretched out in all directions, sometimes lengthened, sometimes shortened, and was not as time and space is now.

So it was that in this time of old, when men were tall as the cedars of Lebanon, and women had children at the age of a hundred, and babies of ten days old stood up and walked, a child had been born at the gates when the sixty-nine men and women entered the city of Pharaoh, as has already been told. And her name was Jochabed.

She grew to womanhood through the reign of Pharaoh, she grew through the reign of Joseph alone, and through the reign of Pharaoh's son, and she grew in the reign of the new Pharaoh. And only then she had a child. And that child was Miriam. She had a second child, and that child was Aaron. And when Pharaoh had placed guards outside the houses to wait for children to be born, that they might throw the boys into the river, she was one hundred and thirty years old. (And indeed some say she was two hundred and six, and others that she was three hundred and fifty-three.) And she had a third child – a boy.

He was born three months before his time, therefore the guards were not yet come. She stilled his crying, so that none knew. Then when the guards had still not come but were expected, she sent his sister Miriam to the river, where bulrushes grew, strong and tall as trees, and people made of them boats to sail the Nile. And it was night.

And Miriam brought back an armful of rushes, and an armful again, and another armful; and they made a boat, a small one. It was an ark like the Ark Noah made long ago when a unicorn and a giant swam behind; but this was a little ark.

They smeared it inside with the soft red mud of the river Nile, and they smeared it outside with pitch to keep out the water. And inside Jochabed placed the sleeping child.

And Miriam laid the cradle in the rushes near the Red Sea. Here were no crocodiles, and the water was soft and calm.

And as the sun rose, came the Princess Bathia, daughter of Pharaoh, with her ladies-in-waiting. And the Princess bathed in the river, while her maidens walked alongside.

"See," said Bathia, "there is something in the rushes."

"It is a box," they said. "No, not a box, but it resembles a box...."

"Bring it to me," she said.

And they lifted the box out of the reeds, and it was an ark, with a baby inside. And they brought it to her. And she said, "The god of the Nile has brought me this gift." And she put out a finger, and touched the baby's cheek. And he turned his mouth to her hand. And she understood.

Then Miriam stood up out of the reeds where she had hidden, and said to the Princess, "Shall I find you a nurse? One who can feed the child?"

"Do so," said the Princess.

So Miriam brought Jochabed, who had not stirred since she gave the child to Miriam to lay in the rushes. And the Princess said to Jochabed, "Nurse this child for me for these three years, and I will give you wages." And Jochabed was filled with amazement, and could not speak, only took the child, her own child.

The three years went by. And Pharaoh believed the child

who menaced him must surely have met his doom by water, as Balaam had read in the stars. (And Balaam had read truly; but the water that spelled his doom would be the water of Meribah one hundred and twenty years later, and not the river that joined the Red Sea.)

Then Jochabed took her child back to Princess Bathia, as she had been commanded; and the Princess gave him a name. He had already many names, from his mother, his father, his sister, his brother; and many more names clustered around him, and each had a meaning. But the name the Princess gave him is the name he is named throughout the world – 'Moses', which is 'drawn out', for he was drawn out of the river.

And it is said in song and story that Pharaoh was amused to see him, and sat him on his lap; and the child reached out and took the crown from Pharaoh's head and set it on his own.

"The dream! Remember the dream!" cried Balaam.

"He is but a little child!" cried Bathia.

"He means to be King," said Balaam.

"He reached for it only because it shone!" cried Bathia.

Then Pharaoh, at the counsel of his wise men, ordered a slave bring two platters, one bearing a piece of gold, one bearing a red-hot coal. "If he reaches for the coal," said Balaam, "it is because he has no understanding, and no destiny. If he reaches for the gold, kill him."

And the child reached up, and he reached for the gold that flashed and twinkled. But God called the angel Michael, and he quickly pushed the child's hand away. Then the child turned to the coal instead which also burned, with a duller glow. And he took it and put it in his mouth. And on that day his mouth was harmed, and he believed himself to be slow and wearisome of speech; but he was wrong.

But the child lived, and grew. Three years in the arms of slaves. And now the years of the Palace, the years of gardens, the years of orchards, of flowers, and pavilions. And the lullabies his mother had sung him still drifted through his head like the shreds of a dream.

Teachers came from other lands for great fees, to instruct him in writing, in mathematics, in medicine, astronomy, philosophy, art. And he learned all the wisdom of the Egyptians, and the arts of the body also, such as wrestling and leaping, and riding. And it is said in song and story he was a youth mighty in words and in deeds.

And he who was the child of slaves and had lived three years among slaves became a man of war for Pharaoh. And he conquered cities and brought back slaves for him, and chests full of jewels, and swift chariots. And Bathia told him that the power of the Pharaohs would one day be his, for he was her son; and Princesses then were powerful in the land.

So Balaam, who had sought his life and given most evil counsel against him when he was a child, became more and more afraid of his might, and fled to Ethiopia, to the court of King Kikanos. And he hoped Moses would forget him.

But it happened that one day Moses rode out in Egypt with his slave behind. And he rode into a part that was forbidden to him, the land of Goshen. And this was where the family of Jacob and Joseph brought their flocks when Pharaoh had said, "Come, all the good things of Egypt shall be yours."

And he saw men and women and girl-children waist-high in mud, treading mud with their bare feet, loading mud into baskets, mixing straw with mud, shaping mud into bricks. And he saw men with whips standing over them.

Now he was drawn to Goshen as a thirsty hart is drawn to water. He came there secretly, many times, though the territory was forbidden him by Pharaoh. He sought to help the slaves as they toiled in the deep slime. But their masters whipped them the harder for his interference, and the slaves cringed away from him and snarled at him to leave them, saying, "Go back to where you came. The whip does not fall on you." And he knew not what best to do, for he was as unable to stay away from them as the panting hart can stay away from the waters where the lion and jackal will also come.

It came to pass that once when he came he saw an Egyptian smiting a slave most grievously. He looked this way and that, and when he saw there was no man, he slew the Egyptian and hid him in the sand.

And he went out on the second day, and he saw two of the slaves themselves fighting together. And he said to one – for he thought in their wretchedness they would help one another – "Why do you do this? Is it not enough that the Egyptians persecute you? Why do you strike your fellow?"

And the man said, "Who made you a prince and a judge over us? Would you like to kill me as you killed the Egyptian?" Then Moses was afraid, and his certainty fled from him.

And the man went to Pharaoh and said, "The one called Moses has killed one of your officers. He is no Prince. He is the child of a slave woman, pulled out of the river."

And Pharaoh sent out men to capture Moses, and they took him before the executioner.

And as the executioner raised his arm to kill him, God struck the sword from his hand with one finger. And Moses fled from the face of Pharaoh, and out of the land of Egypt. And he fled into Ethiopia, where Balaam had fled before him.

THE PLACE OF THE SERPENTS

Now Balaam, Pharaoh's wisest magician, had seen the child of the dream grow into a powerful Prince, skilled in all arts of Egypt, and loved by Bathia. And he had fled to Ethiopia in fear of him. And he gained the trust of the King of Ethiopia; and he spoke in his ear, and the King listened to him.

So it happened that when King Kikanos made war with the Assyrians, and took an army against them, he left behind in Ethiopia Balaam and his two sons. And he said to them, "I leave my country in your charge", for he trusted them.

But Balaam was treacherous, and immediately the King was gone he made himself King of Ethiopia. And he straightway equipped the city so that no-one might enter against Balaam's will, making the walls many times higher on two of the sides, building canals on another side, and on the fourth digging a ditch and filling it with snakes and scorpions.

So it was that when Kikanos had subdued the Assyrians and returned to Ethiopia, the city gates were locked. And seeing the high walls, and the waters, and the snakes and scorpions, he thought Balaam had feared an attack by neighbouring kings and had fortified the city against it for his sake, and he praised him in his heart for wisdom. But the gates of the city did not yield to him, and he called in vain, "Open for your King. I, Kikanos, speak!"

And when Moses fled also to Ethiopia, King Kikanos had been fighting Balaam many years, to gain entrance back into his own city, his own home. But the walls and the waters, and the scorpions and the serpents prevailed over him.

Then came Moses, fleeing from the sword of Pharaoh.

And the songs say he was slender as a palm tree, and his face was like the morning sun, and his strength was equal to a lion's. And Moses found favour with Kikanos, and Kikanos welcomed him and made him commander-in-chief of his besieging armies.

And when it came to pass that Kikanos, still besieging his own city, became sick and died, his men set Moses as King in his place. And in the seventh day of his kingship Moses said, "Go each man into the forest. Bring out a fledgeling stork. And teach it to fly as the hawk flies." And each man did so, finding a fledgeling stork, and training it.

Then Moses said, "Let the young storks be starved for three days." And each saw to it, and let the bird have no food. Then Moses said, "Let each man put on his armour, and let him gird on his sword, and let him mount his horse. And he shall set his stork on his hand. And we will rise up and fight against the city, opposite the place of the serpents!"

And they rose up opposite the place of the serpents. And the ravenous storks swooped down on the serpents and destroyed them. And the warriors blew many trumpets and advanced over the place that had been the place of serpents, and they took the city.

And Balaam and his two sons would have been captured. But they used their magic arts, and rose into the air as the men of Moses entered. And they escaped, and fled back to Egypt.

But Moses was surrounded with honour, and he sat on the throne of Ethiopia, with Queen Adonith at his side, and he reigned in Ethiopia for forty years. And he was a king of wisdom and a friend to Adonith, but no more. So that after forty years in this wise Adonith said, "It is enough."

And she said to the people, "Monarchos, my son and the son of Kikanos, is now full-grown. It is better for you to serve the son of your lord, than a stranger." So Moses left Ethiopia; and the people gave him gifts of ivory and ebony and many treasures.

And not wishing to return to the land of Egypt (for he feared it) he journeyed on to Midian. And in Midian he came to a well, and rested there. And this was the same well where Jacob had once met Rachel; a well that God had created at the beginning of the world for such meetings.

Now the seven daughters of Jethro came driving their father's sheep; and they drew water from the well. And they poured the water into the stone troughs for their father's flock.

But a band of wild shepherds came roughly and drove them away, and they were scattered as sparrows by ravens. And Moses stood up. And he watered their flock. And he helped them and was gentle with them. And they were gathered together and quickly done.

So that when the seven daughters came home, their father said, "How is it that ye are come so soon today?"

And they said, "An Egyptian delivered us out of the hands of the shepherds, and also drew water enough for us, and watered the flock. And he was most gentle to us."

And he said unto his daughters, "Where is he? Why is it ye have left the man? Call him, that he may eat."

Now the eldest of the seven daughters was Zipporah. And she was fair to look upon and pleasant in the eyes of Moses. And it is said in song and story that she took him by the hand, and led him to the joyous tree in the garden of Jethro, the tree that was the Staff that God made on the

Sixth Day of the world. And she said, "My father has told me that he who marries me must first pull up this tree. Many have tried, but the tree devours them."

So Moses took hold, and it came up willingly in his hand, like a dove winging home. And instantly it became a Staff again, straight and unbranching, and fitting easily into his palm. And its colour was again the colour of the sapphire sky, and on it was engraved its one word, one name - All-That-Is. And Jethro said, "You are the man." And he gave him the Book of Mysteries, and the shimmering Cloak also; and it still smelled of a field of apple trees.

THE BLAZE

Now Moses was the shepherd of Jethro's flock; and he knew each animal separately, with its different voice and its different need. And he understood the ways of those who might do them hurt, the wolf out of the woods and the eagle on the crag. For he had the Book of All Knowledge Worth Knowing, and the Cloak with its pictures of all animals made, and the Staff that still smelled sweetly of the Garden of Delight. And he knew the streams that hide in rocks, the leaves that heal, and the secrets of the silent wilderness.

But God still did not speak again to humankind.

One day, when there were eagles in the sky, a lamb strayed out of the flock, and Moses could not find it. Then he saw it, far away, and he leapt from crag to crag to reach it. And the sun burned him, and he was most angry for he was afraid for it. And God still did not speak.

Then as he reached it, he saw it licked the trickle of silver water that ran between two rocks, so eagerly, so thankfully, and his anger turned to pity and love, and he waited till it had drunk its fill. Then he picked it up, laid it over his shoulder, and carried it back to the flock, singing gently like a mother to a child. And God said softly, "I will speak again to these humans I have made."

Now God caused a thornbush to burst into flame, yet the fire did not cause the tree harm which was strange and wonderful. So that Moses stood still and watched, marvelling. Then God spoke out of the fire.

"Moses, there is crying in Egypt. Go and bring my children out."

And Moses stood transfixed. Then he spoke, shaking

his head.

"God, I am a shepherd! I am a shepherd!"

"You have been a shepherd. But now you will bring my children out of Egypt, into a land flowing with milk and honey."

"God, let me stay here. I love these valleys and this mountain."

"You will return here. The mountain will wait for you."

"God, do not be angry but I hear my sheep crying. I must go to them."

"I hear my children crying in Egypt."

"God, they will kill me! Did they not seek to kill me before, so that I fled from them!"

"Those who sought to kill you are dead."

"But why should I return there? Do I need trouble, Lord? Who am I to go to Egypt and tell Pharaoh to let go his slaves!"

"Did I say that? Say to him only this: 'I have met with God, and God said, let my children go three days journey into the wilderness to pray for me.'"

Then God said, speaking faster, "And I know the King of Egypt will not let you go, except I show a mighty hand. And I will smite Egypt with all my wonders. And after that he will let you go.

"And when you go, you shall not go empty. You shall ask of your neighbours and of them that sojourn in the same house, jewels of silver, jewels of gold. And you shall put them upon your sons and upon your daughters. And you shall empty Egypt!"

There was silence. Then Moses said, "They will not believe me."

And God was exasperated, and said, "What is that in

your hand?"

And Moses said, "A staff."

And God said, "Cast it on the ground!"

And Moses cast it on the ground, and it became a serpent; and Moses fled from it in fear.

Then God said to Moses, "Put out your hand, and take it by the tail."

And he did so. And it became a staff again. And God said, "Do that before them, that they will believe that you spoke with me!

"And if they will not hearken to the voice of the first sign, take of the water of the river, and pour it upon the dry land. And it shall turn into blood!"

And Moses stood there, like a sheep in the rain, and he said, "God, I cannot speak well. Do you not remember my mouth was burned when I was a child?"

"Do I not remember! Who caused it to be burned? Who has made man's mouth? Who makes a man dumb or deaf or seeing or blind? Is it not I? Now go! Even Sammael could speak in the mouth of the serpent in the Garden of Delight. I shall speak in your mouth!"

"But who shall I say sent me? They will ask 'Who?' What shall I say is your name?"

"Say 'I Am What I Am. I am the Lightning, the Beetle, the Rock. I am the Moment-as-it-Moves. I am All-That-Is."

Moses was silent.

"Are you deaf?" said God.

"No, God, I am overcome, I have never heard such names before. I do not think they will be much liked.... God, find someone better than me."

"Go there!" thundered God.

The Separating Sea

So Moses rode to Egypt on a little ass. And it is said in song and story that it will be ridden again one day when the wolf lies down with the lamb and none learn war any more and all the trees of the world shall shout for joy; but that is still to come.

From Egypt came his brother Aaron to meet him, and they went together to the Palace of Pharaoh. Now the Palace had four hundred entrances, a hundred on each of four sides. And at each entrance there were sixty thousand soldiers standing, and two lions who snarled and walked back and forth, lashing their tails like whips, so that none could approach till tamers came to lead the lions away.

And God sent down the angel Michael to take the hand of Moses and of Aaron and to walk with them into the Palace; and they were like little children visiting a grandfather. And the lions bowed their heads in greeting. So that Pharaoh said, "Those two old men must surely be magicians."

And Balaam said – for he was once more in Egypt – "O mighty king, if the old men approach again tomorrow, let the tamers loose the lions against them." But when on the next day they loosed the lions, the lions frolicked at the two men's feet, licking their toes and pouncing with gentle joy and rolling in ecstasy like dogs when their master returns home. Till Moses said "Enough!" and the lions rose reluctantly to their feet, and sat obediently.

Now Moses spoke to Pharaoh, saying, "The God of the Hebrews"– for 'Hebrew' means 'those from beyond the river' – "says to you, 'Let my people go, that they may hold a feast to me in the wilderness.'"

And Pharaoh said, "Who is this God? I know not this God. Nor will I let them go."

And they said courteously, "Permit us to go three days journey into the wilderness, lest our God fall on us with pestilence or the sword" (for they were afraid, at this early time, to say "lest he fall on *you*").

And Pharaoh said, "Why do you distract the people from their work? See to your own affairs! Do not meddle with mine!" And he instructed the Egyptian taskmasters, and the Hebrew officers who served under them, to give the slaves no more straw for their bricks, but to force them to find the straw for themselves, and still to make the same number of bricks, on pain of lashings. "They will have no time then to heed lying words," he said.

So was it worse for the slaves. And they said again of Moses, as they had done forty years before, "He puts a sword in the hands of our enemies."

And Moses said to God, "Why are you dealing so ill with these people! Why have you sent me here! Why do you do this! Since I came to Pharaoh to speak in your name, he has dealt worse with them, not better! Nor have you delivered them at all, for all your words!"

And God said to him, "Now will you see what I will do." And he said, "Speak to the people. Tell them I am the Maker of All who will deliver them from bondage, and will bring them into the land I pledged to Abraham, to Isaac, and to Jacob, a land flowing with milk and honey, and I will give it them for their heritage."

And Moses spoke to them. But they had no courage, for there was little breath or spirit in them because of the cruel bondage that was now increased. And they hearkened not, but said, "We are like a poor sheep that has been dragged away by a wolf. The shepherd pursues the wolf and tries to drag the sheep from its jaws; and between the two of them we are torn to pieces."

Then God said, "Speak to Pharaoh."

And Moses said, "God, if I cannot make the people listen, how shall I make Pharaoh listen? Did I not remind you, my mouth was hurt in childhood?"

And God said, "I will tell you myself what to speak, and you will tell Aaron, and he will say it clearly to Pharaoh. There is no problem." And she spoke faster. "And I will harden Pharaoh's heart, and I will multiply my signs and wonders, and Pharaoh will not hearken to you, and I will lay my hand on Egypt and I will make great judgements and the Egyptians shall know that I am the Almighty when I bring my children out!"

And Moses said angrily, "I know that you will deliver them in your own good time, as it suits you! And it is of little importance to you that they are walling up living slaves in these buildings!"

And God only answered, "You will see what I will do."

Then at God's order Moses took up the sapphire Staff which he had leaned on when he kept the flocks of Jethro, and which had grown in Jethro's garden, and which once had been Adam and Eve's, and they went before Pharaoh. Moses cast it down before Pharaoh, and it became a serpent.

And Pharaoh laughed and said, "It is surely the way of merchants to carry goods to a place where there is none of them, not many. Would anyone take brine to Spain, or fish to Acco? Do you not know I am adept in all things magic, and so are all in Egypt?"

And he called for his wise men and his sorcerers and they cast down their rods and they also became serpents. And Pharaoh called for little schoolchildren, and even they performed the same wonder. For when magic had been given to the world, Egypt had been given nine out of the ten parts. And he laughed again.

But the sapphire Staff swallowed up all the rest. Then Pharaoh was angry. And he hardened his heart. And he said, "No, they shall not go!"

Then God said to Moses, "Did I not say so! I hardened his heart!"

Then at God's word, Moses and Aaron went out in the morning, and stood on the brink of the rising river, to meet Pharaoh when he went to the waters. And they took the sapphire Staff, and saying, "Our God said 'Let my people go', and you have not listened," smote the waters. And the water turned to blood. (And it is said in song and story that all over Egypt water changed to blood, in running streams, in cups, even in the very dough they made for bread; and the fish died, and there was naught to drink, and only the water in Goshen still ran clear.)

But Pharaoh said, "I will not let them go," and turned and went into his house.

And God said to Moses, "Now say to Pharaoh, 'If you do not let my people go, I will smite you with thousands of frogs, from the pools, from the rivers, from the canals. They shall come into your house, they shall come into your bedchamber, they shall come into your bed, they shall come into your ovens, they shall come into your mouths, they shall come into you. And so shall it be with your servants also, and with all the Egyptian people.'"

And Moses and Aaron stretched out the Staff, and it was so. And frogs covered the land of Egypt.

But Pharaoh's magicians laughed and said, "We also." And they did also, through their secret arts, bringing even more frogs, who croaked louder than human voices. And they preened themselves.

But Pharaoh called for Moses and Aaron, and he said, "Enough of frogs. Entreat your God to take these frogs away. And I will let the people go."

And Moses said, "Do you name the time. Then you shall share the glory. For at the very time you proclaim, then shall the frogs depart from you." For he was still courteous.

And Pharaoh said, "Tomorrow be it."

And the next day the frogs immediately died, not slowly but immediately, not one by one but in thousands, in the houses, in the courts, in the fields, in the ovens, on the tables, in the beds. And they gathered them together in heaps; and the land stank, and now was silent.

And when Pharaoh saw there were no frogs, his heart was hardened and he said, "No, they shall not go."

And God spoke to Moses, "Now say to Aaron, 'Stretch out the Staff, and smite the dust.' And the dust shall become millions and billions and trillions of tiny insects that shall devour man and beast."

And it was so, and men and beasts were bleeding and swollen. Only in the land of Goshen walked they as always. And the magicians also performed their magic arts, but this thing they could not do for they could not bring forth anything smaller than a barleycorn. And they said to Pharaoh,

"This is the finger of God."

But Pharaoh's heart was hardened, and he hearkened not to them; and he said, "They shall not go!"

And God said to Moses, "Now say to Pharaoh, 'If you will not let my people go, I will send tomorrow strange mixtures of noxious beasts, lions, wolves, bears and leopards, and serpents and scorpions also, and all such as seek their prey in the dark of night. And they shall prowl about you, and about your servants, and about your people; and the houses of the Egyptians shall be lurching with them, the walls all misshapen. And only the land of Goshen where my own people dwell shall be spared."

And it was so. And the noxious beasts prowled in the houses of the Egyptians, and the houses lurched with them. And this time Pharaoh was affrighted, and he sent for Moses and Aaron, and he said, "Go! Hold your feast to your God in this land, as you wished!"

And Moses said, "Not in this land. In the wilderness, three days journey, as our God said, and we repeated to you."

And Pharaoh said, "I will let you go into the wilderness. But do not go far. And entreat your God for me to remove these mixtures of beasts."

And Moses said, "I will entreat for you that the beasts go tomorrow. Only do not deal treacherously with me any more."

And Moses did so. And the mixtures of beasts departed. But God hardened Pharaoh's heart. And he did not let the people go.

Then at God's word, Moses sent a plague on all the animals that remained in the fields, on the cattle, on the goats, on the horses, on the donkeys, on the camels, and on the sheep. And all the beasts in the fields died that were of the Egyptians, but of the Israelites not one. And Pharaoh sent to inquire, and they told him. But God hardened his heart, so that it was stubborn. And he did not let the people go.

Then at God's command, Moses and Aaron took handfuls of soot from the furnace and threw it into the air towards Pharaoh, and fearsome boils broke out on all the beasts that were shut in shelters, and on all the Egyptians also, even on the magicians so sorely that they could no longer appear before Moses. But God hardened the heart of Pharaoh. And still he would not let the people go.

Then at God's word, Moses stretched forth his hand, and there was hail and thunder, and fire that leaped down to the ground. And the fire rested in the hailstones as a burning wick swims in the oil of a lamp. Then was the barley in the ear, and the flax in bloom, so that the hail smote every herb of the field, and broke every tree. Only in the land of Goshen was there no hail or thunder or fire.

Then Pharaoh called for Moses and Aaron and said, "I will let you go."

And Moses said, "I will ask the Maker of All Things that the thunderings and the hail and the fire that runs to the ground will cease, so that you may know that the earth is God's. Yet I know that you and your servants do not yet respect the Maker."

So God put by what remained of the thunder to frighten the Syrians at twilight in a later time, and suspended the rest of the hail to drop on the Amorites in years to come. But when the fire was no longer flung from the sky, and the thunder and the hail ceased, Pharaoh hardened his heart and did not let them go.

Then Moses and Aaron went to Pharaoh and said, "The God of the Hebrews says, 'How long will you refuse to humble yourself before me? I tell you, let my people go! Do you not, I shall bring tomorrow locusts to cover the face of the earth, such as neither your fathers nor your fathers' fathers have seen, and they shall eat all that remains to you from the hail and the thunder and the fire. And your houses shall be filled with them, and the houses of your servants, and the houses of all the Egyptians.'" And they turned and went out from Pharaoh.

And Pharaoh's servants said to him, "How long shall this man be a snare to us? Let the grown ones go, that they may serve their God. Knowest thou not yet that Egypt is destroyed?"

So they brought Moses and Aaron back to Pharaoh. And Pharaoh said, "Go! Serve your God!..." Then he said, for he was cautious, "But tell me, who are they that go?"

And Moses said, "Our young ones and our old ones, our sons and daughters, and our flocks and herds; for we must hold a feast unto our God."

And Pharaoh said, "No! Not the young ones also!" And he drove them from his presence in anger.

Then at God's word, Moses stretched out the Staff. And the East wind blew upon the land all that day, and blew all the night. And when it was morning it brought the locusts. And they covered the face of the whole earth, so that the land was darkened, and there did not remain any green thing, either tree or herb of the field, through all the land of Egypt.

Then Pharaoh called in haste for Moses and Aaron and said, "Entreat your God to take this away from me." And God called the West wind, and it took up the locusts and drove them into the Red Sea, and not one remained in all the land of Egypt. But God hardened Pharaoh's heart, and he did not let them go.

Then God told Moses, "Stretch out your hand towards heaven, and there shall come darkness, a darkness which may be felt." And Moses did so. And there was darkness in the land for three days, and no-one saw another though he were next to him, and none dare rise from his place but lay down motionless for all that time, lest he be lost. But in Goshen there was light outside and inside the dwellings.

And Pharaoh called to Moses and said, "Go then! Take your little ones also. Only leave your flocks and herds."

And Moses said, "Our cattle must go also. There shall not a hoof be left behind, for with them we serve God."

But God hardened Pharaoh's heart, and he said, "I will not let them go!" And he said moreover, "It is enough! Get you away from me! Take heed you see my face no more!"

And Moses said, "I also wish it!"

Then God said to Moses, "Only one plague more will I bring upon Pharaoh and upon Egypt, and after that he will let you go. Nay, more - he will thrust you out of his house altogether!" And God told Moses what he must say to Pharaoh.

And Moses said to him, "Thus saith the God of Heaven: 'At midnight I will go out into the midst of Egypt, and all the first-born in the land of Egypt shall die, from the first-born of Pharaoh that sits on his throne, to the first-born of the maid-servant that is behind the mill, and even the first-born of the cattle. And there shall be a great cry throughout all the land of Egypt, such as there has been none like it, nor shall ever be again. But against the children of Israel shall not a dog whet his tongue.

"And all these, your servants, shall prostrate themselves before me, and beg me, saying 'Go! Go swiftly, you and all who follow you!' And we will go!"

And he went out from Pharaoh in great anger. And God said to Moses, "But he will not hearken." And he hardened Pharaoh's heart.

And Pharaoh said, "I still will not let the children of Israel go." And the hour moved towards midnight.

Now Moses bade the children of Israel get ready for their leaving. They marked their doors so that God, smiting all the first-born, would pass over their houses. And they ate their last meal in Egypt, in haste, with bread that had no time to rise, with their shoes on their feet, and their staff in their hand; and none went out of the door of his house.

And Moses went to seek the bones of Joseph. For long ago, as Joseph lay dying, when he was still the great Revealer of Secrets, he had said to his brothers, "When you go to the land which God swore to give you, the land flowing with milk and honey, take my bones with you."

And because Pharaoh knew Moses would not leave Egypt without them, he took them from the grave where they waited, and he hid them. And Moses sought them.

And it is said in song and story that he came upon Serah, she who as a little child had sung the song to Jacob four hundred years ago. And Serah put in his hand the silver cup of Joseph, with which he had revealed secrets, and said to him, "Come." And she took him to the River Nile, saying,

"In this river, at this point of the river, Pharaoh threw the box of Joseph's bones, all sealed in lead by his magicians, that it might sink to the bottom. This I know."

And at her telling, Moses cut four flat pieces from the cup of Joseph. On one was engraved a lion, on another a bull, on the third an eagle, and on the fourth a human being. And he threw each in turn into the river, crying, "Joseph, Joseph, the time has come! Only for you do we linger! Come! Else we are free of our promise!"

He threw in the lion. He threw in the bull. He threw in the eagle. And when he threw in the human being the leaden box at last burst eagerly to the surface of the water. And Moses took it, and it was light as thistledown in his arms. And Moses hastened back, for it was nigh to midnight.

And it came to pass at midnight, God smote all the first-born in the land of Egypt. And there was a great cry in Egypt, for there was not a house where there was not one dead. And Moses thought in his heart, "These are the people of Bathia whom she loves, and she took me from the river, and loved and taught me, and I owe my life to her," and he was sore distressed, for she was dear to him.

But death had passed over the houses of the children of Israel and left them alone, for they had marked their doors.

And Pharaoh rose up in the night, and it was as if the firm ground beneath him had turned to the mire of the brickfields and his foot could not stand in an even place, and he called for Moses and Aaron, and he said, "Rise up! Get you forth from among us! Go! Serve your God as you have said! Take your flocks and your herds!.... And bless me also." (For he was afraid.)

And all the Egyptians gave them jewels of silver and

jewels of gold, and their own raiment, and they put them upon their sons and daughters as God had foretold. And the Egyptians said, "Go! Or we are all dead men."

And they left Egypt, two million of them on the march, with their children, and a mixed multitude besides. And they left in the light, openly like free people.

Then, when they had gone, Pharaoh said, "Am I mad that I have done this! Shall I set free all who rebel against me!" And his mind veered round like a weather-vane, and he called for his chariot-riders, and he pursued them with six hundred chariots drawn by fast horses, and three picked charioteers in each, and many warriors also.

And the children of Israel looked, and the Egyptians were to the north of them, and the mountains were to the west and the south, and eastwards was the sea. And they cried out to Moses, "Were there no graves in Egypt, that you have taken us here to die? Did we not say to you, 'Leave us alone, that we may serve the Egyptians?' Always you put a sword in their hands to slay us!"

And Moses said, "Fear not. You see the Egyptians today, but you shall see them never again. God will fight for you. Stand still and hold your peace."

And God said, "Am I to do everything, and you all stand still? Tell them to go forward, and forward, right up to the edge of the sea, and then forward more. And do you lift up the sapphire Staff and stretch it over the water, and the East wind will blow and the water will divide. And those still living in Egypt will know that I have slain Pharaoh and his host and his chariots and his horsemen and have fed them to the little fishes, and I will be in great honour!"

And Moses stretched out the Staff. And an East wind

blew, the same wind that brought the flood the day God unplugged the stars, the same wind that blew through the Tower of Babel scattering words, the same wind that drew the locusts to devour Egypt, the same that would one day destroy Samaria and with it the whole kingdom. The wind blew.

But the sea was angry and heaved itself, saying, "I am three days older than you, O man, for I was made on the third day of the world, and you not till the sixth. Do you not tell me what to do!"

Then twice again Moses urgently commanded the sea. And twice more the sea replied, "Do not command me, young one!"

And Moses cried out to God, "Do you speak to it!"

And God said, "If I now ordered it to divide, it would be in such terror it would not again return to its former state. Order it again, and this time I will set just a little of my own strength at your right hand, and that will be enough to compel it."

And when the sea saw the little of God's own strength standing at the right hand of Moses, it hastily divided. And as the wind parts the corn, the wind parted the sea. And not the waters of that sea alone, but the waters of all the seas, and all the water on heaven and earth, in wells, in pitchers, in little goblets, and in the curving cups of flowers, even the drops of dew on the grass and the tears on the cheeks of children – all divided at that same moment.

And the waters of the Red Sea reared up like horses, and made a wall on the right hand and a wall on the left. And the two walls were hundreds of miles high. And the people went forth into the middle of the sea on a path of dry land.

This the Egyptians saw, and they raised a fearsome shout, and went in after them into the midst of the sea: horses, chariots, and horsemen. And when the children of Israel reached the shore, the Maker of the World said to Moses, "Stretch out the Staff again, so that the waters come together!"

And Moses stretched out the Staff, and the wind changed, and the walls of water plunged down, and the waters were one. And the waters were one in all the seas of the world, and in wells, and pitchers, and little goblets, in the curved cups of flowers and in the drops of dew and in the tears on the cheeks of children. And God toppled the chariots and the horsemen and the horses and all the hosts of Pharaoh into the sea.

THE MOUNTAIN THAT SHUDDERED

And the people stood still on the further shore, amazed. And they saw the pearls, washed into the seaweed, and the emeralds winking on the sand, and the sapphires like blue sky reflected in dewdrops. For the chariots had been rich with treasure. And they began to gather them up, to add to the store the Egyptians had already laden on them; for they thought this was freedom.

But Moses cried, "On! On!" and would suffer them to take the swords and spears only, and the arrows and javelins, such as they might need to use against enemies. And they were angry. And they said to him, "Is not Pharaoh dead? Why are we still fleeing? Let us return."

But he said, "The sea has opened for you. Now it has closed."

Three days they marched, angry. They marched through the wilderness of Shur where there were scorpions, and the snakes were so venomous that if a snake but slithered over the shadow of a flying bird, the bird fell dead. And there was no water.

And the people cried out against Moses. "Were there not graves enough in Egypt, that you brought us to die in the wilderness!" And they pulled their children to him, dragging them by the arms, and thrust their little ones on to his shoulders, crying, "Give them to drink!" And they said, "Always he made things worse!"

And they went on to Marah, which means 'bitter', where water flowed beneath their feet. But when they tasted it, it was bitter, and they vomited it. And they cried out again against Moses, saying, "It would have been better to have died at the hands of the Egyptians!" And they picked up stones to hurl against him, and to kill him. And he cried out to God.

Then God said to him, "Take up a laurel branch, for is not laurel bitter? Cast it into the waters, and the bitter waters will be sweet. Did you not read the Book of Mysteries when you kept the sheep of Jethro, and had time?" (For there it is written 'Turn bitter to sweet by adding bitter'; when they who know not the Book would add sweet.)

And Moses said nothing, but picked up the bitter branch and threw it in. And the people drank, and gave their children to drink.

And they moved on to Elim, and then into the wilderness of Sin; and they had no food left. And they cried aloud, saying, "Would that we had died in the land of Egypt, when we sat by the flesh-pots and did eat bread to the full, and cucumbers and melons also! But you have brought us into this wilderness to die!"

Then God said in anger to Moses, "I will cause bread to rain from heaven each morning. And at dusk I shall bring them meat."

So it was that at even, quails hurtled from the sky like a blizzard of snow. And God was so fierce with the people that many were knocked senseless by the storm of it; but it was meat for them.

And in the morning, dew lay on the ground, and when the dew was gone, it left behind it white flakes like fishes' scales, but round as coriander seeds, and tiny as hoar frost on the ground. And the people said, "What is it?"

And Moses said, "This is the bread God told you of. You shall gather it each morning, and it shall taste to you like wafers made with the sweetest honey, or cakes baked with fine oil, or whatever you most remember and long for. But you shall gather one day's portion only."

So the people gathered it. But some gathered much and stored it; and the next day it was rotten, and crawled with worms. And Moses said, "What is this you do? Why are you greedy? Why do you not trust? Did I not say gather only a day's portion? Each day it will fall anew for you." So they ceased to store it, and had faith in each day.

But on the sixth day they found in their hands twice as much. And they brought it to Moses, and said, "We did not seek to store it. It was not our doing."

And Moses said, "It is for the seventh day. Tomorrow there will be none in the fields. For when God made the world, she rested on the seventh day, and celebrated all that was already there, and brought nothing new."

So every sixth day they stored what was left till morning, and it did not rot. (And they called it 'Manna', which is 'What is it?', for so they cried when first they saw it, for it was unknown to them. And its only other name is 'angels' bread'.)

Then they journeyed into Rephidim. And there was no water. And they fought Moses, crying, "Why have you brought us out of Egypt to kill us?" And they took up rocks.

And Moses cried out, "God, they are ready again to stone me!"

And God said, "Take up once more the sapphire Staff. And stand before the rock at Meribah, and smite it. And water will spring forth." And Moses smote the rock with the sapphire Staff and water came out, enough for all; and those were the waters of Meribah, which would one day cause his death. (Had not Balaam been told so by the stars?) But that tale will be told later.

And this was when Amalek came, a king and a mighty magician, thinking to crush them as a bear crushes a lamb between his jaws. For he knew by his magic art that the people were faint from thirst, and weak from strife, and that certain days favoured him. And he came with a mighty army. And the people were not fierce against him, for they were fighting among themselves and against Moses, saying, "Let us return to Egypt where we ate and drank to the full, and the huge grapes hung like tassels! Here we will die!"

So did Moses call to Joshua, son of Nun, who served him, saying, "Choose men! Go out and fight Amalek. As for me, I will stand on the top of the hill of Horeb holding the sapphire Staff."

And Joshua chose men, and went out to fight, while Moses, with Aaron and another, went up to the top of the hill. And Moses held up his hand with the sapphire Staff. Then did Joshua prevail. But when Moses let the Staff down (for he was eighty years old, and tired, and his arms heavy), then did Amalek prevail.

So Aaron and the other took a stone and put it for him to sit. And he sat thereon, while the two stood on either side and held up his hands, and they became as a young man's hands, steady and strong.

Now strove they equally, Joshua and Amalek, like two pans of a scale that match each other. And as the armies fought, the shadows lengthened. So that Moses was afeared of the coming of the night, for evil might be done in the darkness, and he cried aloud, "Hold back the sun!" And lo, the sun stood still.

Then did Joshua, seeing the sun no longer drove his chariot down the sky, sent forth a torrent of arrows that hissed like angry serpents. And above the hissing and the crying of Amalek's hosts, Moses sat on the Hill of Horeb, the sapphire Staff raised like an unfurled banner. And Joshua conquered.

Then did the sun remember its work, and it straightway fell, sweetly and swiftly like a nut falls down from a tree. And the two who had upheld the hands of Moses now let them fall. And his hands trembled for the blood was thin in them. And Moses spoke to Joshua, saying, "Some day the sun will stand still at thy voice as today it did at mine." And they left Rephidim.

Now came they at last to the wilderness of Sinai. In this wilderness was the mountain of six names, where Moses had once kept the flocks of Jethro, and it was the mountain about which they had once asked leave of Pharaoh.

Now the people stood at the foot of the mountain. And the mountain shook, like an animal shaking its shagginess and rising to its feet. And thunder rolled and crashed, and lightning cracked the sky as if the heavens would fall in jagged pieces, and huge rocks of hail fell on the mountain, as large as children's heads. And the mountain, risen to its feet, flamed with fire, and smoke wrapped it round. And in the tumult, a horn sounded out, long and high.

And it is said in song and story that all the kings of the earth came in fear to Balaam, the wisest of the Egyptians, saying, "Is this again a Flooding of the World? Shall we perish?"

And Balaam said, "Go home again, fools. The Maker of All said to Noah, 'I will never again destroy the world with a flood."'

But they were still afraid, and said, "Is this again Destruction with Fire?"

And Balaam said, "And the Maker said, 'Neither will I destroy it by fire.' Go home again."

And they said, "What is it then, the lightning and the thunder and the hail and the fire, and the trembling and the rising of the mountain?"

And Balaam said, "It is their God who will give the Laws of Living to the world. The Maker will speak at one and the same time in all the seventy languages the world knows. Listen, and you will understand your own."

Then was there a silence and a stillness such as never was known both before and since. The wind dropped, and no bird cried, and every leaf was motionless on the stem. Even the ants ceased their scurrying, and stood like painted marks. And God spoke. "I have brought you out of the house of bondage." And God spoke out loud the first ten laws of the Free.

But the people at the bottom of the mountain were much afraid, and said to Moses, "It is enough. If there is more, God may speak it to you, and you shall tell us, quietly." And they drew away.

So Moses climbed the mountain, and God spoke the rest of the Laws to him alone, in seventy languages at one and the same moment, so that the seventy nations of the world might hear it at one and the same time, not the living only, but also the dead and all those yet unborn. And each understood what he had heard in his own particular way, and in his own particular time and his own particular land would do whatever he had understood.

So one law said, "You shall not kill." And one law said, "You shall love your neighbour as yourself." And one law said, "If you meet your enemy's ox or his ass going astray, you shall surely bring it back to him." And one said, "You shall not muzzle the ox that treads the corn." And one law said, "What you do not wish to be done to you, do not to others." And another said, "Do not oppress a stranger. For you know the heart of a stranger, since you were strangers in the land of Egypt."

And for forty days and nights in the cloud on the mountain Moses tried to learn them all. But what he learned each day he forgot each night; and what he learned each night he forgot each morning. And he said to God, "It is in vain. There are six hundred and thirteen laws. I am but Moses."

So God said, "I will write them down." And she took two tablets of sapphire, and letter by letter and word by word wrote down on them the six hundred and thirteen laws for Moses. First the ten that he had said out loud; and they covered all the two tablets. Then in between the lines, God wrote the rest.

The Long Wandering

There are many stories of Moses, and how he led the children of Jacob and Joseph nearer and nearer to the Promised Land, and how all the time they murmured against him, saying, "Why did you take us from Egypt where the fish leapt freely into our nets, where the juice of the melons was like honey to our parched mouth!", forgetting the lashings and the mud and the children walled up alive.

It is said that even Miriam and Aaron, his sister and brother, began to speak spitefully against him, taunting him that he had once sat beside the Queen of Ethiopia; so that the people mocked and said, "A prince of Egypt! A King of Ethiopia!"

And when he rose early in the morning, they said, "He goes to gather the best of the manna before we wake"; and if he held back they said, "He is so full of secret hoardings he has no need to waken."

And they picked up rocks to hurl against him, so that later he said to God, "My life has more often been endangered by them, than by our enemies!"

And over and over, ten times, God grew wrathful with them and said, "I will destroy them utterly!"

But Moses said, "Were they not slaves only yesterday! Why did you set them down in a land of slavery if you wished them to behave like the free! Give them time."

It is said in song and story that in their journey through the wilderness they came upon the giant Og, who had ridden on a unicorn behind the ark of Noah hundreds of years before, for time was different then. And he had promised Noah he would serve his children and his children's children and all their generations, faithfully and for ever; but he lied.

And now he was King of Bashan, and a declared enemy. And the children of Jacob and Joseph entered his city at nightfall when it was dark. And when the morning came there was still no light, and they cried out, "Our enemies have built a mountain in the night to bewilder us." But the dark was Og. For he sat on the top of the wall of his city, his legs dangling down to the ground, and his shape blotted out the sky.

Then, it is said in song and story, Moses took his sapphire Staff, and it became a Sword as it did once for Methuselah, and grew as tall as himself. And he leapt his own height up into the air, and he reached up at the same moment with his sword, so that the point of his sword was three times his height above the ground. And the very tip of his sword scratched Og's ankle, for Og's foot was large and high. And Og started, and lost his balance, and fell. And thus Moses straightway killed him.

At last the people came out of the wilderness to the River Jordan. And now they were at the very borders of the Promised Land. But still they hung back, saying, "Let us first send men before us to spy out the land." And they did so.

And this was the time of the first-ripe grapes, so that those who went to spy out the land brought out a cluster, carrying it on a pole between two of them. And they brought out also pomegranates and figs. And they said, "Good is the land, a land of milk and honey, and of tinkling brooks and fountains, a land of wheat and barley and vines and olive trees."

But the people murmured, "We have heard there are

giants there." And they cried out and wept, saying, "Would that we had died in Egypt! Would that we had died in this wilderness!"

And of them all, only Joshua, son of Nun, and Caleb his comrade, murmured, "It is true we saw some of great stature. But we are stronger and many more than they and we need not fear."

But the people said, "Let us return to Egypt now! Let us choose a captain and return!"

Then was God filled with anger. And he said, "You are slaves still! You are not fit to enter the Promised Land – and you will not! You shall wander in this wilderness for forty years, till all who are today full-grown, and who are still slaves, have died. But your children shall be a new generation. And they shall go over the River Jordan with Joshua and Caleb."

And so it was. They wandered in the wilderness for forty years. And after forty years the new generation came again to the mountain of the thorn, the mountain of six names which most call Sinai. And they cried out, even the second generation, "We shall die of thirst! Why did you make us come out of Egypt, the land of our childhood, to bring us to this evil place, wherein is no seed, no figs, no vines, no pomegranates, neither is there any water to drink?" And the heart of Moses for a moment of time ceased to beat, as if a hand had suddenly seized a sitting bird.

And when God said to Moses, "Take up your rod and speak to the rock, and they shall have water," Moses was full of rage, and of doubt of the people.

And the people shouted, "The rock! The rock!"

And Moses shouted back to them, "Which rock do you

want, you rebels! This rock? That rock?"

And they shouted back, "What matters it! For a miracle, any rock will do!" And Moses was seized with rage and grief, and he turned to the nearest rock. And the rock had been waiting since the beginning of the world for Moses to speak to it, and it was ready to give, to play its part, joyously.

But Moses raised his Staff, and struck it, once. And one drop of water came out, like a tear. And the people jeered. And he smote again, furiously. Then water poured out of the rock, in a torrent.

And the rock said, "Why did you strike me?"

And God said, "I said speak to it. It was waiting for you."

And Moses said, "The people of the new generation angered me."

And God said, "They were children in Egypt. And they were thirsty. Do you not remember the lamb that you once climbed after?"

And Moses remembered.

And God said, "Moses, it is time for you also to die. You are losing faith. You will not enter the Promised Land."

And Moses said, "Maker of All, that is unfair."

And God said, "Moses, Moses, you are old. You are one hundred and twenty years old this day."

And Moses said, "My eyes are not dim, nor my strength abated. It is not fair. Ten times you said you would destroy the people, and ten times I pleaded for them. Was it not I who said 'Give them time to love freedom'?"

And God said, "You were impatient. You were violent."

And Moses in his heart said, "God, have you not been impatient and violent with us?"

And God knew what was in his heart, and added, "You are tired and old. See, you have taken forty years just to go through this wilderness."

And Moses cried, "But God, it was you! It was you who said we must take forty years, so that those who knew slavery died."

And God said, "Moses, friend, you will see the Promised Land. It is only that you will not enter. I will show it you from the top of a mountain, its brooks and its waters and its fountains. Not only the Promised Land! The day before you die I shall even show you the whole world!"

But Moses said again, "This is not just, God. It is not fair."

And God said, "Moses, Moses, who said I must be just and fair?"

And Moses said, "You, God. You said you were just and fair!" God shrugged one shoulder and smiled sadly.

And the people watching below saw Moses climb slowly up the mountain, four and a half thousand feet to the very top of the mountain, as the day wore on from morn to even. And they saw him stand at the top and look north, over the palm trees of Jericho and all the mountains beyond, into the whole of the Land of the Promise. And they watched him looking.

And as the dusk came down, they watched as he turned, and moved towards a valley. And he never came forth from the valley, though they continued to watch, crowding and jostling like starlings roosting, nor was he ever seen again, nor his body found.

And they said, they who had picked up stones to hurl at him, "There is none like him, for he and God spoke mouth to mouth, as one speaks with a friend. And we who are left, how shall we live now?"

But it is said in song and story that when Moses stood at the top of the mountain, and the people could not hear his words, he said to God, "I will not die! I have given to Joshua the Cloak and the Book and the sapphire Staff as you told me. I have taught him all I know, as you told me. But I will not die! For it is not fair." And he turned, and went into the valley, and walked in anger and sadness through the night towards the grey gleam of the Dead Sea.

And in the morning he came to some stone-cutters. And they were cutting out a space within a rock. And he stopped and said, "What is this you are doing?"

And they said, "The king has thus commanded us. He has a precious treasure which he will lay in this room, to hide it from human sight."

And they were courteous to Moses, and gentle. So because it was near noonday, and the sun was burning over their heads, he asked leave to shelter inside. And as he lay down there, the leader of the workmen offered him an apple, that the juice might refresh him.

He took it gladly. And it smelled like his Staff and the Cloak and the ancient Book, like fields that God had blessed, with strong-smelling spices. He bit into it. And in an instant he died. And God wept.

And Jochabed, still living, though now hundreds of years old, wandered through the world, calling to all living things, "Have you seen my son? Do you know where he is?" And no-one has ever answered, for no-one knows.

THE ONE WHO COMMANDED THE SUN AND MOON

The memory of Moses stayed with the people, as the leaf on the tree still trembles after the bird has flown.

For though Moses had given to Joshua the Cloak and the Book and the sapphire Sword, as God had bidden him, and had taught him all he knew, when the people came to Joshua with their questions he could not answer them; and they despised him. "He is a fool!" they said. "He knows nothing!"

And they cried aloud, "How shall we that are left live now? Give us Moses again, Moses who spoke to God mouth to mouth, as to his friend!" For they had already forgotten how they raged against him.

And Joshua said, "God, what shall I do with this people? They despise me, and speak against me!"

And God said, "There is no problem. Are you not a soldier? Give them wars. Then they will forget their questions." And this was easy for Joshua, for he understood war. And did he not have the Staff that becomes a Sword, with which Methuselah had slain many demons, and Moses had slain the giant Og as he sat on the city wall turning morning into night?

Then said Joshua to the people, "God has said to me, 'Cross over the River Jordan, and I tell you that every place that the sole of your foot treadeth on, that do I give you. I will not fail you nor forsake you. And in three days you shall inherit the land.' So God spoke to me."

And the people stood in the shade of the acacias, and looked out over the river. And in front of them, they saw the lovely city of Jericho, and heard, limpid as shepherd's pipes, the tinkling sounds of brooks and streams and running water, and saw the kingfishers dipping for fishes, and hummingbirds hanging dizzily over lilies, and heard the nightingale that sang day and night - the land flowing with milk and honey that they believed was to be theirs. And their questions died on their lips, and they longed for it.

Then Joshua, the man of war, sent two men to cross the river and spy out the land. And these men stopped at the house of Rahab.

Now Rahab was one of the four most beautiful women in the world. (Sarah, who was first called 'My Princess' and then called 'Princess of All', whose hair was like an eagle's wing, was her equal, and equal too one day would be Abigail and Esther; but they were not yet born.) And it is said in song and story that Rahab's house was a house where men went constantly in and out. And the spies mingled with them.

But the King of Jericho had watchers also. He sent to Rahab commanding, "The two men that have newly come to you, bring them forth! They are two of the escaped slaves and they are spying out the land!"

Then the heart of Rahab fluttered and almost stopped, like a bird that is caught suddenly in the hand. For all the people of Jericho had whispered of the frogs that had filled people's mouths, they had spoken in fear of the dying of the first-born, and in terror of the Red Sea dividing. And she said to herself, "Their God has given them our land."

So, in her fear for her children and her father and mother and all in her house, she hid the men.

And she answered the King, "Most gracious one, indeed it is true they came to my house. But they went at the time of the shutting of the gate. Let your men follow quickly. They will surely overtake them."

And the King's men followed as she said. And once they were far away, she brought the two up on the roof where flax was spread in the sun to dry, and she hid them among the stalks. And she whispered to them, "All people here know how the waters parted for you. We know that your God has given you the land. There is no spirit left in our people here because of you. They melt away before your coming, and mourners go about the streets hearing the rattle of death.

"So since I have dealt kindly with you, remember my doing, and therefore deal kindly with my father and my mother and my brothers and sisters and the children and all who are with me."

Then she let them down by a scarlet cord through the window (for her house was against the city wall), saying, "Go to the mountains. Hide there three days. Then safely go your way. But remember me. Remember me and my house."

And the men whispered to her, "Keep the scarlet cord. When our God gives us this land, bind it to this same window. Whoever is with you in your house with the scarlet cord, that one shall be safe."

And it came to pass, the people of Jericho drew every bolt, and locked every gate. And they waited in fear, for outside their gates were those for whom the sea had divided, and not only the sea but all the waters of the world.

Then in the mists of morning the people saw through the cracks of their windows the wraiths of a silent army circling the city wall. No soldiers' shouts, no clatter of arrows, no clash of arms, no screams of horses, no running feet, no oaths. Only silence, and the silent circling movement like a silent spell. Once round the city.

Then, suddenly, from strange trumpets, a long hoarse screeching cry that hung on the air like the mist itself screaming. And silently the men melted away.

And it was like the first howling of wolves on the edge of a listening village that howl and trot softly away. Or like the shriek of an owl that scoops out the cringing heart of the hearer.

All that day long, the people of Jericho waited, unable to look in each other's eyes for fear. All day, nothing. Nothing to see. Nothing to hear.

Then the next dawn, the wraiths again, slipping in out of the mists. One silent circling of the city. No shouts, no clash of arms, no human voices. Only the silence, and the shapes like ghosts, circling the city in the mists of morning. Then one unearthly scream from the trumpets... and they were gone.

The next the same. And the next. And the next. Six days in all of silent ghostly movement, till the air quivered with waiting for that to come which came not, till the warriors of Jericho were crying out at the soft chirrup of a bird, and a dead leaf fluttering past their window stopped their women's hearts.

On the seventh day, again the ghosts, with their single silent circling. Then a change. A circling again. And again.

And again. Seven times in all this day, the silent circling. Then the scream, longer, wilder, mightier than any other morning. Then shouting, shouting, shouting, as if the very air rained blows on the terrified people with unseen clubs, and Joshua crying over and over, "Shout, all ye! Shout! For God has given you the city!" And there was a trembling of all the people, that grew into a terror from God. And the walls of Jericho fell down.

And the army of Joshua walked into the spellbound transfixed unresisting city, and destroyed all that was in it. Only the family of Rahab, as had been promised, were left alive, in the house that showed the scarlet cord.

And still Joshua gave them wars, one war after another, so that there would be no more questioning.

And in those times God remembered the days when the people were slaves in Egypt and Pharaoh would not let them go, and God had made great hailstones, and thunder that roared out, and fire that leaped down to the ground with a whipcrack. And that when Pharaoh had said, "Enough. I will let them go!" God had told the hailstones to suspend their falling, so that they hung in the air, hovering like kestrels, waiting for the command to re-enter time.

And now the command came. For all the Amorite Kings came out of the mountains to fight against them. And God remembered the hailstones. And he said, "Now fall!" And obediently they let go the hold of all those years, and fell. And so great was the rage and force stored up in them by the waiting, they killed more men than were killed by the sword. So says the song and the story.

But night was nigh and Joshua sought for a way to hold

back the dark, being afraid that victory might slip away like a snake into the shadows. He remembered a different battle at the end of a different dying day, and saw in his mind a hillside, and heard again Moses, holding the sapphire Staff above like an unfurled banner, command the sun to stand still. And the sun had indeed stood still obediently. And time itself had waited.

And he remembered how Moses had said to him, "Today the sun has stood still for me, as one day it will stand still for you."

So Joshua lifted the sapphire Staff that Moses had given to him, and cried out now with a loud cry, "Sun, stand still!" And emboldened by his own voice as by strong wine he spoke again and cried, "And stay moon, stay!"

But the sun cried back, "Lo! I move because I sing! My singing drives me and I must move!"

"Then stop your singing!" cried Joshua.

"I cannot stop my singing. For my song is the celebration of the world, and I forever celebrate!" thundered the sun.

"Only stand still for me and hold back the dark," cried Joshua, "and I will sing the celebration in your stead!"

And Joshua sang. And his voice was the voice that had shouted once over the shouts of his men, "Behold! God has given you the city! God has given you the city!" Till the walls of Jericho had split asunder, and fallen in ruins.

And now with that same voice he sang. And at his voice, the sun stood still; and not only the sun but the pale moon also. And time stopped.

And only when the battle was won, did Joshua cease his singing. Then the sun and the moon roused themselves and went their separate ways across the sky, and the order of day and night again took up its course. So tells the song and the story.

But one day one came to Joshua, as once many had come to Moses, and he asked for an answer to a question.

"Why", he said, "did God forbid us iron tools?"

And Joshua said, "I know Moses told you this. He told you that when you build places of glory for God, you must not use iron spikes or spades or hammers. It is because God does not love iron."

And the man said again, "Why?"

And Joshua said, "It is because we make swords and spears out of iron, and use it to kill." And the man cried out, "But is it not God who tells us to kill? Are these not God's wars?"

And Joshua said, "The people say I cannot answer questions like Moses. Yet even Moses did not answer this one."

And now the rift between humankind and the rest of the universe grew even wider. The Cloak, the Book, and the sapphire Staff slid from the people's memory. And for many years there were no songs, no questions, no more searching for answers.

So it came to pass, when Joshua was one hundred and ten, and life was shorter than in the days of Eden, he died. And it is said that though the mountain where he lay blazed in anger, no-one came to bid him farewell, for the people were cherishing their new possessions in their Promised Land.

THE WISE CHILD

And now, for many years, no-one sang of the Three Gifts, that God had given Adam and Eve when she sent them out of the Garden of Eden (though she had meant them to live there for ever) - the Cloak of snakeskin, the sapphire Staff, and the Book of All Things Worthy to be Known.

And after Adam and Eve, Seth of the columns had them, and Methuselah and Noah, whom the Phoenix addressed so courteously, and Nimrod of the seven thrones, and Abraham and Isaac, Esau and Jacob, and Joseph of the rainbow coat and the dreams, and Moses, who spoke to God as to a friend, and Joshua the lone man, who knew only war and did not answer questions. But now, when the people began to have kings (for they had said angrily, "We want no more prophets to berate us; we want kings, like other nations, to wage wars for us"), the Three Gifts were forgotten.

For not even King David is said to have held them, David, who when but a child killed a giant whose height was that of two men, one on the shoulders of the other, David who was the Maker's beloved (for so means his name), not even he had the Cloak and the Book and the sapphire Staff.

But his son Solomon had them. This is how it is told, in song and story.

When David was a hundred years old, he said to God, "What day shall I die?" For he already knew he would be a hundred years old when he died. Is it not said in song and story that Adam, when with Eve at the riverside he first read the Book of All Knowledge Worthy to be Known, had read of David, who was not yet born, and had said to God,

"Who is this wondrous man, this warrior, this lover, this maker and performer of songs, whose harp plays him messages in the troubled night, whom the people love for he goes in and out before them, who is he, O Maker of All? And how many years have you given him?"

And God had said, "That is David, my beloved. I have given him seventy."

And Adam cried, "O Maker of the Universe, give him more! Give him thirty of mine!"

So God answered David who had now had the hundred years, "You are to die on the Sabbath. Not the day before, for that is a day of study, and I do not wish you to lose it. And not the day after, for I have already appointed Solomon to be king from that day."

Now David knew that no-one would die while they were studying, for learning is a kind of growing that is the very opposite of dying. So every Sabbath, all day long, he studied, so that God could not take him. Until at last God said to the Angel of Death, "Enough!" and he told the Angel what he must do.

So the Angel sat in a tree, and there he made a noise – a flapping and a rustling and a shivering, such as a cluster of birds make when a predator is nigh. But there were no birds and no predator.

Then David, still holding his book and reading from it and studying and taking care, took a ladder and set it against the tree to discover the reason of the noise. And as he stepped on each rung of the ladder, he kept his eyes on his book and never ceased studying, so that the Angel could not take him.

But the Angel put out a hand, and he loosened the next rung of the ladder. And as David put his foot there, carefully placing it, the rung shifted, and he stumbled and caught his breath and cried out. And in that one moment he stopped studying. And the Angel laughed and straightway took him.

That day was a Sabbath. And the next day Solomon was king.

He was twelve years old. And already God had given him just a little of his own wisdom, but not too much, as he had given Moses just a little of his own strength, but not too much.

For it is said, in song and story, that when David still reigned as king, and Solomon was still a child, the servants of David had sat down to eat, and chicken's eggs that were boiled had been placed before them. And one of the servant boys was so beset with hunger that before his companions had even turned to see what lay on theirs, he instantly cleared his dish. And he was ashamed that he had done so. And he turned to his neighbour, and asked softly for the loan of an egg, that he might lay it on his plate, and be as others.

Willingly, nay eagerly, his companion gave him one, and added, "On the day when you repay me, give me also what it would have earned." But being ill at ease and desirous of quickly merging into the throng, the boy did not dwell on the words or much hear them.

Year followed year, until the one who had sat beside him accosted him and asked repayment. The boy gladly gave him an egg. But the other cried, "Would you thieve from me! That be far from you! Where is what it would have earned?" And the boy remembered that he had not paid attention on that day.

So warily he said, "Speak then. What would it have earned?"

And the other shrugged and said, "In one year, another chicken. In two years, eighteen more. In three years, one further one for each of the eighteen. And by now" – but the boy turned swiftly from him and said in anger, "We will go for judgement to King David." For David heard the great and the small, and the old and the young, for all were worthy alike to him.

And they went by the gate of the Palace, no longer talking, being enemies, and they met a young child, Solomon, who said, "Go you for judgement to my father?" And they said they did. And the child said, "Pray tell me, on your return, what he speaks to you."

And in his Palace they told David, and David considered and said to them, "It is a true debt. It must be paid."

Thus they returned, one jubilant, one bitter and angry. And the bitter one said to the child Solomon, "So spoke your father."

But Solomon who had a little of God's wisdom standing by his heart said, "There are many kinds of wisdom. Know you the ploughed land where the regiments of the King pass by? Go there and hide. When you hear them coming, rise up and take a handful of boiled beans and strew them on the ground.

"They will rein in their horses and gaze at you, and say, 'What game is this?' Tell them you sow boiled beans. And when they mock, as they will, and say, 'Who has heard of boiled beans bringing forth fruit?' do you say, 'He who has heard of a boiled egg bringing forth a chicken.'" (And God laughed, for he liked the human being.)

So the boy in his sorrow did as the child Prince told him, for what more could he lose? That day and the next, as each of the King's regiments passed by, the same act, the same answers to the same questions.

And all began to speak of it, not the soldiers only, but all of the people, one telling another and turning the words over as a babe with unaccustomed food will turn it on the tongue.

Until at last the word reached David. And he sent for the boy and said, "Who told you to act thus?"

And the boy was afraid, and said, "No-one. It was I only."

And David said, "No. I hear the voice of Solomon."

And the boy said, "Yes. It was he."

And David sent for the child Solomon and said, "Yours be the judgement. You are the wiser."

That was the young child Solomon, whose name means 'The Peaceful'. And now he was King. And when he began to reign, there were songs again of the Book and the Cloak and the sapphire Staff, though how the Three Gifts came to him no-one knows, only that they had come to him as a wandering dove comes home to its nest.

THE THREE LOAVES

And God said to Solomon in a dream, "What shall I give you?"

And Solomon said, "I am but a child. Give me wisdom." For he believed once he had wisdom, all else would come of itself.

Now it came to pass soon afterwards that a certain king died, leaving four sons who did not know who was the true heir. And they came to Solomon for counsel.

And Solomon said, "Take the dead body of your father, set it upright, and fire your arrows. Whoever transfixes the heart of his father, that one is the next true king." Immediately did three of them set the dead king upright, and seize their bows and aim their arrows. And they transfixed their father. But none transfixed his heart. And they shouted with anger, and argued and beat each other about.

But the fourth son was amazed, and stood rooted to the ground and moved not. "Rather would I give up the throne than do so," he said.

And Solomon said, "He that would not do so to his father is the true son and heir, and your true next king." Thus was Solomon's wisdom.

And it happened again, for there are many songs and stories, that two women came to him for counsel. They dwelt together in one house and in the past night each had had a child. But when they awoke that morning one child was dead. And each cried that the living child was hers and the dead child was the other's. "She rose at midnight and took my child from beside me while I slept, and she laid it against her breast, and she put her dead child beside me," cried one. And the other cried, "Nay, she did so. The dead child is hers. The living is mine."

Solomon heard them and he said, "Bring me a sword." And he said, "Fairness is all. Divide the living child in two, and give one half to one, and one half to the other."

And one of the women said, "Yes, do so. That is just. Let it be neither mine nor thine, but divide it."

And the other's heart trembled and she cried out, "No, my lord, my lord! Hold your hand! Give her the living child!"

And Solomon said, "Give to that one the living child, the one who would not let it be slain. She is the mother." So was his wisdom that God had given him.

And it is said in song and story that a poor woman came to him, weeping. Each day, she had baked three loaves, two for the poor, one for herself. The day she came to him, a stranger had knocked at her door. "My ship has been wrecked," he said, "my comrades have perished, my possessions all tossed into the sea! I alone was thrown on the shore. And for three days I have made my slow way here. And I am exhausted, famished." And she had given him a loaf without question.

Then she had sat down to eat. But another stranger knocked, saying, "I was caught by bandits on the road. I escaped into the forest. For three days I have eaten only roots and herbs and berries that the birds have left. I have forgotten what bread tastes like." And she had given him the second loaf, unquestioning.

Again she had sat down to eat, and a third knocked. "I have been kept a prisoner by evil men. Only three days ago, I broke my bonds, and escaped – but without food. Give me bread." And she gave him the third loaf.

Then had she said to herself, "Perchance if I shake it well, I will get enough grains from the empty sack to make a tiny loaf for myself." So she shook it by the two closed corners, and then carefully swept the grains together, and carried the little handful to the mill; and there it was ground to flour.

Carefully she put the little bag on her head and began walking home. But of a sudden the wind sprang up, and a gust whipped the bag away and it was gone. And she wept as she told Solomon. And she said over and over, "Why has this befallen me? What did I do?"

As she spoke, three merchants entered Solomon's hall. They came quickly up to the King. "Lord and King," they said. "Here are seven thousand gold pieces. Give these to any deserving."

And Solomon said to them, "Why? What has happened?"

And they said, "Lord and King, we were sailing in our ship, indeed approaching the shore. And our vessel was filled with costly merchandise. But suddenly we saw there was a leak. We had nothing to fill the hole. Our boat began to sink. And all we could do was to pray. And to the Maker of the Universe we vowed with all our heart that if we reached shore safely, we would give away one tenth of all the merchandise.

"How it came about we know not. But the water then ceased to enter. In that instant, something stopped the hole. And we safely reached the shore. There we calculated our goods, and these seven thousand gold pieces are exactly one tenth, as we swore. And here are they." And they laid them down before him.

And Solomon said, "Do you know where in your ship the hole was, and do you know what it was that stopped it?"

And they said, "No. In our anxiety and then in our joy and then in our eagerness to come here and pay our debt, we did not investigate."

And he said, "Go now, and do so." But already he knew the answer. And they returned, as he knew they would, with a small bag of flour.

And Solomon gave the old woman the seven thousand gold pieces. And he smiled, and said, "You see, you did not need to weep. God did not forget you."

So it was that his wisdom far excelled the wisdom of Egypt. And all the kings of the earth came to hear him. And when he sat on his throne and gave judgement, if any stood before him with falsehood in his heart, all the animals of gold who stood on the six steps of his throne would cry out, shrieking or roaring or screaming, each after its own true living fashion. And terror would seize those who had thought to bear false witness, so that they cried within themselves, "We must speak the truth or the world will fall!"

But his wisdom was not only of human beings. For he knew the truth of trees, from the noble and lofty cedar of Lebanon that takes its proud steps to the sky, to the sprig that springs from the cracked wall and is no more than a finger-length. And he knew the truth of beasts of the wild, and beasts of the field, and of birds and fishes, and the tiny creatures that creep and crawl.

And when the kings of the earth sat at his table, eating of delicacies from all corners of the world, and the court musicians played on the violins of his father David so that the low strings growled with joy and the high ones cried with love, Solomon would summon to dance before them beasts, birds and reptiles, and demons and ghosts and spectres of the night. He called them by name, and they came, freely and unfettered.

And with wisdom, as he had thought, all else followed, and his life blazed with riches and splendour. So it came that the throne he sat on was of ivory and gold. And the names of the great ones were carved on it, such as Adam and Noah and Moses and many besides for they were all one family, and he remembered them.

And it is said that on each of the six steps stood twelve eagles and twelve lions, and round about them a lamb and a camel, a dove and a peacock, a cat, a hen, a panther, an ox and a wolf. And all were of pure gold.

And in his stables were four thousand horses, with barley and straw for all, and all of twelve thousand horsemen, and many gold chariots, and he raced with them for joy and delight. But when he rode on affairs of the world, then did he ride on an eagle, or on the wings of the wind, or on his shimmering Cloak embroidered with pictures and still smelling of Eden, which he spread like a carpet and sat upon, and thousands of men-at-arms sat with him. For space, like time, was still different in those days. Is it not said in song and story that King Solomon and his men flew from Damascus to Media in one day, breakfasting in one and supping in the other?

And when he married the daughter of Pharaoh of Egypt and the whole land rejoiced, hundreds of maidens came with her bringing musical instruments of different kinds and played on them day and night with fingers that twinkled with jewels. And above his bed the Princess spread a canopy studded with diamonds and pearls like the dark star-studded sky, so that whenever he woke he should think it was night, and stay with her.

And all the days of Solomon, the family of Jacob and Joseph dwelt safely, every man under his own vine and under his fig-tree. And there was neither adversary nor evil, only rest.

Then Solomon said, "I will build a house for God. For she has given me wisdom and peace, and three most precious gifts, a Cloak, a Book, and a Staff. Rare stones will men bring me from Ophir, and gold and silver from Tardish, and red sandalwood to make musical instruments that I will play like my father David, singing my own songs. And ships will crowd to bring them, and agile apes swing from the awnings, and peacocks stiffly stalk their decks. Only" - and he was perplexed - "with what shall we cut the stones to build the house of glory?" For it was known that God had forbidden the use of metal, since metal is used for swords that kill. And with what else could they cut the stone?

Now Solomon had many counsellors. And one was so exceeding old that his words were as soft as a young chick in the reed-bed; but Solomon would stoop and bend his ear to him. And the counsellor told him that on the eve of the very first Sabbath, when God had made the Staff for Adam and Eve and the bow for Noah, and had put them by till they should enter time, so also had he made a worm no bigger than a barleycorn. It was called the Shamir. And it could split rocks. And now its turn was come.

Now Solomon had the Book of Knowledge, that told of all things to come, and of meeting angels, and capturing demons. And he took up the Book and turned its pages. And when he had read his fill, he turned to Benaiah his friend, who was beautiful as the evening star, and he gave him some wool, some skins of wine, and a ring with a chain that was signed like the Staff of Adam and Eve with the one name, All-That-Is. And he sent him to find the worm. For so had he read.

So Benaiah who was called Benaiah the Beautiful went forth across the desert to the barren mountain-top, where lived Ashmodai, King of Demons. In this his own mountain Ashmodai had dug a well, and each evening when he came back from the far ends of the earth, he would look to see that the huge stone he kept thereon had not been touched (for it was fastened with his own seal). And when he saw that the seal was unbroken, he would drink.

Benaiah took care not to touch the stone. But he made a little hole, and through this he drained dry the well. Then the hole he carefully stopped with the wool. And he made another hole, and through this poured wine into the well. For so Solomon had instructed him, from the Book of All Knowledge that is Worth to be Known. And Benaiah hid nearby and waited.

And in the evening came Ashmodai back to his mountain-top. And first he looked to see none had touched the seal on the stone, and it was just as he had left it when he went to the far edges of the earth. Then he drank deep at his well, for he was parched, and his mouth dry as a smoked wineskin that longed for the cool caress of water.

But the wine made his mouth only drier, and he drank again. And again and again he drank, each time thirstier, each time drinking again and drinking deep, till his eyes closed, and he fell to the ground, and he slept.

Then came Benaiah, out of his hiding-place. And Benaiah threw round the neck of the sleeping demon the chain that was threaded with Solomon's ring with its one Name All-That-Is. And he settled himself comfortably to wait for Ashmodai to open his eyes.

Then Ashmodai awoke - and he saw the chain with the ring round his neck, and he ground his teeth and he spat! And spitting and snarling, he was pulled to his feet, and stamping and leaping he was dragged over the ground, and trees were ripped from the earth, their roots writhing in the air like serpents; and he was forced before Solomon. And Solomon said, "Speak, King of the Demons, speak! Where is the worm no bigger than a barleycorn?"

And Ashmodai slashed at the air, till Benaiah shook the chain to mind him of his slavery. Then his slashing ceased, and he said through his teeth, "Wisest of mortals, the worm called the Shamir was given to the Prince of the Sea, and is his treasure. And because he cared for her he entrusted it to the woodcock, that she may split rocks with it, and place seeds therein with her long beak, that they might grow into plants to sustain her. And she holds it carefully under her wing, and keeps it with her always, except each night when she returns it to him, for she knows it is the Prince's own."

Then Solomon smiled at Benaiah. And he gave him this time a small box, a piece of clear glass, and again some wool. And Benaiah the Beautiful again crossed the desert, and again searched for a mountain.

And at last in a hollow in the ground he found the woodcock's nest. And in it were four fledgelings, alone. For she herself was away from the nest, seeking food for them.

And Benaiah covered the nest of fledgelings with the piece of glass, and he hid, waiting. And he watched the sky.

First he heard a whirring. And then he saw the woodcock's wings like a daytime owl black against the sky. And she flew down to enter her nest and feed her young ones as always. But she could not, for the glass prevented her. She could see them, and she saw the inside of their gaping mouths, and the frantic fluttering of their wings, and she heard their tumult, and she drove her beak against the glass. But she could not reach them.

Then in her wild distress she remembered the worm no bigger than a barleycorn, that the Prince of the Sea had entrusted to her. And she took it out from under her wing, and placed it on the glass, for her young ones were crying to her with their wide scarlet mouths.

And at one and the same instant, like the thunder crack that comes with the rain and the wind, there was the shattering of the glass, and the shout of Benaiah, and the clapping of the wings of the woodcock as she flew up in the air. And in triumph Benaiah snatched the worm.

And so it was that the stone was cut for the House of God with the worm no bigger than a barleycorn. It is said that all stones were made ready before they were brought to the building, and neither hammer, nor axe, nor any tool of iron that brings with it death, was heard in the House.

But though the woodcock had saved her children, she had lost the treasure of the Prince of the Sea, who had entrusted it to her in his kindness, that she might grow plants in the rocks to sustain herself. And she gave a wild desolate cry, and in her grief killed herself.

So says the song and story.

The Lilies and the Nightingale

The Princess of Egypt who hung over the bed of Solomon the sky and stars, that he might think it was still night and stay with her, was but the first. For as time went by, Solomon had one thousand wives. And all their heads were balanced on deep silver necklaces like eggs in egg-cups; and their ankles jingled like bells in the wind.

And each one murmured, "Come, be my guest tonight. My table is laden with delicacies, and my mouth is sweeter than honeycomb. What a banquet I have for thee. Come." And their voices were low and insistent, like bees on the vine blossom.

But every eventide he said to himself, "Would it were morning!" And every morning he said secretly, "Only one evening with each, and it will take three years off my life."

And as he walked in his garden he heard the lilies murmur one to another, "We are more beautiful than he."

And the nightingale, as he passed, said to her beloved, "That one has a thousand wives, but none love him as I love you." And his heart growled within him, for he was like one whose mouth was crammed so full that he tastes nothing.

Now this was still the time of the seven years' building of the temple, and Solomon had sent to all kings and princes, saying, "Send me your best artisans, your quarriers of costly stones, your builders, your engravers, and your jewellers, and those who make garments all of blue, with pomegranates of purple, and scarlet on the skirts, and tinkling gold bells hanging. Send me your delicate spinners of silver filigree, and those also who are strong and can carry the mighty trunks of the cedars of Lebanon. Rich will be their reward." And many heard and streamed to Jerusalem, City of Peace, for the gold and a share in the glory.

But one artisan of great worth said to his Prince, "My wife is as lovely as a gazelle that skims the mountains. And men are sinful. I would not leave her even for the nearest town. Shall I then, for the sake of gold, work in Jerusalem!"

But his Prince said, "I cannot refuse Solomon. You must go."

And the man clenched his fists, and wished to say more. But he was silent, and went home to his wife. And she saw the inward turning of his face, and the blindness of his eyes, and she questioned him lovingly. And at last he told her the reason. And she smiled, and said, "I will give you a talisman."

She gave him a tiny glass bulb, and inside was a glimmering coal and a strand of cotton. And she said, "As long as this cotton does not catch fire, you will know no faithless flame has caught my heart." And she put the talisman on a chain round his neck, and kissed him; and thus he went to Jerusalem.

Now it was the custom of Solomon to come each day to see how the workmen progressed. And he saw the talisman round the man's neck, and said, "What is this?" And the man told him.

Then Solomon secretly summoned two handsome youths, and he sent them to the house of the artisan's wife; for he wished fiercely to see the talisman change. He watched it eagerly day by day, as he came to check the progress of the work. But it did not change. (For in truth she had received the young men courteously, and given them food and drink, and shown them to their room and locked them in.)

And Solomon was perplexed and angry that she was true to her man. And not able to leave it alone, he went himself to the village, unknown.

She received him with honour. She bade him sit, and put many dishes before him, cakes, and milk, and little golden melons. And at the last she gave him a plate of boiled eggs, each painted a different colour.

"I have eaten enough," he said.

But she said, "Taste them, only taste them, my lord and king."

And he said, "Why call me lord and king?"

And she answered, "Your kingship shouts its name. I knew you when you entered." And she said again, lightly, "But pray tell me, my lord, how these eggs taste."

So at last he ate a little of each one; and he said, "They taste alike."

And she said smiling, "With women it is the same, my lord. Like them we are only differently painted. It was truly not worth your while to travel so far."

And a warmth spread through him, and he said, "So blessed you are, you shall be as a sister to me."

And he gave her a gift from his person, costly and beautiful. And he returned to Jerusalem and gave the artisan ten-fold wages, and said, "Go home. You have a jewel. Be happy with it."

And the two and Solomon had friendship from that day, and he spoke often with them and prized their love, their love for each other and their love for him. But he was still not satisfied and he did not learn.

Now Solomon had a daughter Kaziah whom he loved;

and she was as beautiful as the lilies that grow by the waterside. One day he read in the stars that she would marry a poor and destitute lad. And he resolved he would prevent it.

So he summoned builders to build a high tower on an island in the middle of the sea; and he summoned sailors to row the Princess there. And he summoned seventy men to guard her, and there left her.

Now the destitute boy who was to be her husband but did not know her went out into the world to earn his living. One night as the light was fading, he crossed a field. A cold wind arose, and broken branches and straw flew by him in the darkness, unseen and hurtful. And the rain fell as if it passionately longed again to rejoin the sea. He searched the dark for shelter. And in a lightning flash he saw the carcass of an ox, not yet picked clean by the birds. He crept inside it, and it cradled him, and he fell asleep.

Now it happened that some hours later an enormous bird swooped down, and carried off the carcass, thinking to devour it somewhere undisturbed. And still the tired boy slept. And the bird flew to the tower of the Princess, and descended on to the roof of it. And it dug out the flesh of the carcass, and when it was eaten clean flew away. And the boy still slept.

In the morning he awoke. And in front of him was a Princess. And she was as beautiful as a lily by the waters, with eyes as blue as fireflies on a night of velvet. And both were full of astonishment, and spoke to each other wonderingly, and touched each other with frightened fingers that grew less frightened.

And the Princess took him to her apartment and gave him food and drink, and showed him where he might wash and bathe himself and put on clean apparel. And as they talked she discovered that though poor, he was learned.

"Unhappy boy," she said. "None can leave this high tower, nor cross the sea." But he was not unhappy. He stayed with her, and they fell in love. And in only a little while the Princess asked him to marry her. So he took a small knife, and gladly cut his hand. And in his blood he wrote their marriage contract.

Time passed, and at last the guards discovered them. With trembling hands they wrote a message to Solomon, and wrapped it round the foot of a sea-bird and sent it forth over the water. And it circled over the palace and cried out till the King himself threw open the doors, and read that his daughter whom he had left in a high tower surrounded by water was married. And in a rage he flew to the tower on his shimmering Cloak. And he saw it was the boy of the stars.

The Queen of Sheba

It is said in song and story that night after night the kings and princes who had come on their snow-white camels, or in white-sailed ships that sped through the waves like swift doves to their nests, sat down to dine with Solomon. Birds and beasts brought them delicacies from Tyre and Tarshish in dishes of pure gold. The court musicians played on the violins of his father David, and the singers sang; for were not the songs of Solomon one thousand and five? And ghosts of the night danced for their pleasure, like wreaths of mist in the valley, or smoke of the camp-fire.

When his guests lay down in sleep, Solomon surveyed those that called him lord, his beasts and his birds and his spectres of the night. And he saw that the hoopoe was not there, and he was angry. For the hoopoe is rosy as spices of cinnamon, and its wings are like the black bars of a praying shawl that lie devoutly on its back; and he was accustomed to the colours and the pattern of its presence, which now was not there. And in anger he called aloud its name.

Scarce had the sound merged into its own echo, and the echo into silence, when the hoopoe appeared. "Be not angry, my lord and King," the hoopoe said. "For three whole months have I covered the world in your service. All that time I have taken neither food nor drink, and only this moment have I returned. In your honour I went, my lord; for I wished to seek out any country that does not acknowledge you king. I have found such a land. Its name is Sheba.

"There the gold we love is scorned, and dust is valued more. There silver is nothing and mud is greater prized.

Not one knows how to fight there. Not one how to strive with a spear. Not one aims a bow and arrow. Not one kills. And upon their heads they wear garlands woven in the Garden of Delight. And the ruler is a woman – the Queen of Sheba."

Solomon's eyes grew narrow, as a hunter who measures the distance to a grazing gazelle. "I have heard of her," he said; for he had heard the songs and stories that whispered she was Lilith, Lilith of the beginning, who still walked the land, though it was long since the time of the Garden of Delight.

"Oh give me permission, lord and king," cried the hoopoe, "to journey to Sheba. I will fetter its minor kings with chains. I will bind its minor rulers with iron bands. I will seize the Queen of Sheba, and bring them all before my lord, and have them kneel to you!"

Solomon considered. For a while he was silent. Then did he summon scribes. And they wrote a letter as he spoke it, and they bound it to the hoopoe's wing. And like a giant butterfly leaving a flower, the hoopoe rose, and flew across the sky; and the other birds followed. And Solomon sighed, as one already weary.

Far away, the Queen of Sheba rose in the dawn to worship the sun. The gleam of the day spread from the east, and stained the river at her feet, and she lifted her face to the sky that soon would be pearl and rosy like a dove's breast. But lo, the sky grew black as night again. And for one moment she was affrighted, till she saw it was the coming of thousands of birds.

Then from this huge black cloud that curtained off the dawn, one flew down, one bird alone. Slowly it descended, and as it sank to earth, it called like a hollow flute, as if it summoned her. And she came, curious. And she saw the message tied to its wing, and she took it.

"From me, King Solomon. Know that I am King of the beasts, of the birds in the air, of the fish in the sea, and of all demons, spirits, and spectres of the night. All Kings of the East and the West come to salute me. If you will salute me also, I shall show you great honour, more than to any king. If you will not come, I shall send out my kings who are the beasts of the field, my riders who are the birds, and all my legions which are demons, spirits, and ghosts of the night. The demons will kill you in your bed, the beasts will kill you in the field, and the birds will eat your flesh."

The Queen of Sheba considered also, as had done Solomon. She thought, sadly smiling, "This is Solomon the Wise, whose name means Peace." Then she too sent out a letter.

"From the land of Sheba to the land of Israel is a journey of seven years. But as it is your wish I visit you, I will hasten, and be in Jerusalem in only three."

Then she gave commands to fill her ships with the finest of fine woods, with pearls and jewels and spices. And she summoned six thousand youths and maidens, all born in the same hour, and clad all in purple they stood side by side on the deck. And sweet and strong, the scent of the balsam she brought carried far out to sea and over the curling waves to Solomon; and he lifted his head like a stag, and knew her coming.

Then sent he to meet her Benaiah the friend of his right hand. And Benaiah was beautiful to look upon, like the flush in the sky at daybreak, like the evening star that outshines all other stars.

When the Queen saw him, she descended from her chariot to do him honour. "Why do you thus?" asked Benaiah.

"Are you not then King Solomon?" she said.

And he answered, "No, I am not the King. I am only his servant."

So that she said, "But you are yourself a star. He must indeed be the blazing sun."

And the songs and the stories tell that Benaiah escorted her to the dazzling House of Crystal, where King Solomon awaited her. And she had never seen such a wonder, made by the hands of men, so that she cried out, for Solomon seemed to her to walk on water; and as she came towards him, she lifted her skirts to keep them dry. And he laughed and put out his hands to her.

And it is said in song and story that they sat near to each other, and played with riddles and answers to riddles, and exclaimed, and laughed together. And she said, "You are greater even than they told me. And they told me so much, my senses swam as in a rose garden."

And he said, "I would give one hundred opals for a direct look from your eyes."

And she laughed and said, "I have heard Cain also measured and counted." And his brow grew dark, and he would have leapt to his feet, but she said, "Oh be not angry, my lord," and laughed again. And her laughter was drowsy as a bee at noon, and his limbs melted and he could not move.

And she gave him presents she had brought - many talents of gold, and of spices a very great store, and many most precious stones, for she knew he would prize them. And he gave her all her desire.

And he said to her, "You do light again my lamp, and put a new song in my mouth." For she seemed to him to smell not of palaces, but of saffron and sweet calamus and cinnamon, and a field of apple trees. And his tongue was like a bee that slips into the flower, and her nectar was cool and sweet.

Black and comely was their child. When the time was come, he would be Prince of Ethiopia, which one day would be named. And he would be the first of the black Falashas, who are known to this very day. But all that was yet to come.

They named the child Menelik, which is 'son of the wise one'. And Solomon loved him more than any child he had had of the Princess of Egypt, who had brought the canopy of stars to put about their bed, that he might never know it was morning, and more than any child he had had of the thousand others, each one a princess also.

How long they two were together, no songs sing. But they sing that the tighter he held her, the more she wished to go; for she was a queen equal to his kingship, and some say she was Lilith of the loose golden hair and was not to be bound.

So it came that at last she said, "Dear my lord. This be your land, and that be mine."

And he said, seeking still to hold her, "But you are my dove."

And she answered, "Doves are caught by nets, yet they return to their nests. Yours is a goodly land. But in mine the boughs that bend and then return, as the boughs in all lands do bend and return, do not send forth arrows but scatter blossom."

And she said, "What has passed is sweet. But now it is morning."

So did she take her leave of him, she and her companions, and he watched till her ship was as small on the horizon as an ant on his garden wall, and still he stayed and watched till there was nothing, and still he stayed.

At last did he come and sit alone at the entrance to his palace. And before him two birds sang and caressed each other with their beaks. And he watched them and listened. For he understood their language, and he was intertwined with love as they were.

And he heard one say to the other, "Who is this man seated here, beneath these trees?"

And the bird-wife answered, "Do you not know? He is the man whose name and fame fill all the world! He is Solomon."

And the bird said, "Oh, he who ordered the building of these palaces! Why, my beloved, did I but wish it, I could by just fluttering one wing overturn them all, and they would be as dust."

"Do it!" And she chirped and chirruped. "Do it! Show me!" And she laid her head on his shoulder.

And it is said in song and story that Solomon, whose heart for a while had been so heavy all gold had turned to grey, listened, amazed and amused. And he crooked his little finger and beckoned. And the bird, terrified and ashamed, fluttered the short way to him, and whispered, "Let not my lord be angry. I spoke this only to please my wife, and look great in her eyes."

And Solomon smiled within himself, and he spoke sternly to the bird, and sent him back to his wife.

The bird-wife was perched with her head on one side on a twig a little way off. And she said, "What did the King say to you? What did he want?"

And the bird puffed out his chest and said, "He had heard what I said, and he begged me not to destroy his palaces, for he values them. And he was so pitiful and afraid, I promised."

Then in a flash was Solomon angry, for he remembered how he had boasted also, how he had boasted to the Queen of Sheba of his power. He remembered Adam who had driven Lilith away with the weight of his might. And he remembered his letter. And in that swift anger at himself he turned the little birds to stone. And their chirruping was stopped for ever.

And there they stand to this day, two small birds on the Dome of the Rock in Jerusalem, frozen in stone; though Solomon himself and all his glory have tumbled into dust. But that is yet to be told.

THE END OF THE KINGDOM

So time passed, moving further and further from the day when God, having made all things, made lastly the Man-and-Woman-in-One; and God had smiled at it, and said, "Do not be proud, for even the tiniest insect that dances on the air is older than you."

Now one day Solomon sat on his shimmering carpet, with a hundred thousand armed men around him, balanced on the arms of the wind. And he cried in jubilation, "There is none like me! I am Solomon!"

The wind dropped. Forty thousand men fell from the carpet into emptiness. And Solomon in fear cried out, "Return O wind, return!"

But the wind said, "You have grown too proud, Solomon."

And Solomon cried, "I was wrong. I will be more humble. Only return, return!" And the wind puffed and coughed a little, for it was still brooding.

And then it returned, saying, "I will blow. But remember, do not boast."

Now all those hundreds of years ago when the mountain of six names rose like a shaggy beast to its feet and hailstones fell as large as children's heads, Moses gave to the people a little command among all six hundred and thirteen; and it is still writ down today in the books. And it says, "When it comes to pass that you have come into the Land of Promise and you want kings because others have kings, do not take a king that gathers up a multiplication of wives, or a multiplication of horses, or a multiplication of riches, or boasts he is better than his fellows."

And this command that was still then in the air like a breath that is breathed, flew up to God and said, "I am despised. Remember me!"

And God nodded, and said, "I remember you. You are right to complain. For this, I will rend away the kingdom from Solomon. Only I will not take it wholly yet, for I loved David his father; to take it wholly, I will wait till he is dead."

But God straightway summoned Ashmodai, King of the Demons, and ordered him, "Descend immediately into Solomon's palace. Take the Book, the Cloak, the Staff that is sometimes a Sword; and take the ring. Look as Solomon, and sit on his throne."

And Ashmodai laughed with delight. And he at once descended on the palace and seized the Book, the Cloak, and the Staff, and he snatched the ring from Solomon's finger. And being most marvellously pleased and full of energy, he swallowed down Solomon, then, stretching out his wings, one touching heaven, one touching earth, he spat him out four hundred miles away.

Then Ashmodai sat on the throne in the exact likeness of Solomon, and was content for a while. And what he did in the likeness of Solomon astonished the people, most of all his thousand wives and his mother Bathsheba, so that they said wonderingly, "The King is not himself." And a few added, "It is strange that though the air is languid and the lilies droop on the stem, the King wears stockings, which thing he has not done before." (They did not remember then that the feet of demons are hard to disguise.)

But, far away, Solomon (like Jacob, years ago, fleeing from the brother he had cheated) begged his bread from door to door. Three years he wandered, weeping. And when a door opened he would say piteously, "I am Solomon, King of Israel," and they would laugh and the door would close. And through the mire of the streets and the market-places and the valleys and the desolate places of owls, he wandered, crying, "I was a king in Jerusalem." And they taunted him and jeered; and he was hard put to find food until one said, "It is a madman," and gave him sustenance, and a little clothing.

One day he saw a rich man, and whispered to him hoarsely, "I was King in Jerusalem."

And the man stopped, looked at him closely, then said, "Yes! You are Solomon! What has befallen you?"

And the man took him to his house, showed him where he might bathe, and laid a rich banquet before him. And he said, "How I remember your brilliant courts, when the beasts and the birds and the ghosts of the night danced before us, and the golden bears and lions roared like living creatures at any who spoke not the truth, and you gave out judgements that touched all the kings of the world with wonder. And your thousand wives with their tinkling feet and their veils and their gauze robes, who each entreated you to dine with them, how sweet it was then...." And Solomon cried and left him, and could scarce grope his way out for grief.

The next day he met a poor man, and again he said, "I was King in Jerusalem. I am Solomon." The man believed him, and invited him to his home, though it was a poor one, he said, and small and dark.

Solomon thanked him and went with him gladly, but said, "Only, I pray you, do not speak continually of my past glories, for the memories blind my eyes with tears."

"I cannot speak so," said the man. "I never saw your

court. I can give you only a dish of herbs. But I will solace
you and bring you some comfort for I believe in truth that
God will give you back your kingdom." (And it is said that
ever afterwards Solomon who had supped with kings
remembered the dinner of herbs, where love was, that was
better than a banquet.)

Three years he dragged himself from door to door, ever
more weary; and he came into the house of an old woman,
who thought he was but a beggar. And he wept therein
from eve till the morning. All night he wept, and she asked
him why. But he would not give her reason. For he said,
"I cannot tell you. You will not believe me." But she pressed
him. And still he continued to say, "You will not believe
me. And I am ashamed." But still she continued to question
till at last he said, "I am King Solomon."

And she said, "How then did you lose your kingdom?"

And he told her, "One day Ashmodai appeared and
seized my Cloak and my Book and my Staff, and snatched
the ring from my finger and hurled it into the sea."

"That is a strange story," said the old woman. "Strange
to any hearer, but most strange for me; for yesterday I bought
a big fish in the market, and when I cut it open I found
inside this ring." And she took it from her shelf.

It was his ring.

At the sight of him, it flashed and sparkled, seeming to
cry out to him, as if sight were sound.

With her gnarled hands she placed it on his finger.
Immediately he was swept as by a great wind to the gates of
Jerusalem, and thence to his throne.

And humbly now he reigned again, till his death.

But when he felt his death approaching, he feared lest

it become known to the demons, who had always warred against him even when he had dominion over them and forced them to be builders for him and bringers of stones and rare herbs. For he was afraid of what they might do, Ashmodai above all, when they knew his strength was ebbing, and his eyes failing him, and his breath precious.

So he sat on his throne as if all was well with him, and he leaned on a beam of wood as if he slept. Day by day, he leaned a little further forward. And all thought he was still sleeping. And leaning thus, he died, and his breath departed, and none knew.

After many months it happened that a woodworm came to live in the beam. It gnawed through the wood of the beam, sprinkling the powdered dust over the golden eagles. And slowly the King toppled from his throne.

Then the demons knew Solomon was dead. And they were filled with a wild zest for destruction. And in glee they began to lay waste all that he had done and all he had forced them to aid him in doing. And the kingdom was rent away as God had said it would be. For he had forgotten that the tiniest insects that dance in the air are older than human beings, and mankind should not be proud.

And naught was heard of the Cloak that was also a flying carpet, or the Book of all mysteries, or the Staff that could be a Sword, for all of two thousand years. And all that time there was not one song or story.

The Cave and the Sleeper

The Three Gifts waited for their time to come, as a watcher on the side waits for the right moment to slip into the marching music, as a reveller waits for the right moment to join the dancing pattern, or a child to slip into the skipping rope-twirling throng. And the two thousand years passed.

Then one night, a door was flung back, and a sleeping man strode out into the dark. Unseeing, unhearing, he strode a bold straight path into the wilderness, as a bee flies straight to a flower. Dry wings rattling, the bats dropped from branches. Snakes hissed over the ground with menacing tongues. Shadows deeper than shadows shifted nearer to him. But the man strode boldly by, seeing and hearing nothing.

And God looked after him, and removed all trees from his path, and filled in all deep hollows tight with tamarisk trees, and put the great towering rocks to one side for him.

He strode unfaltering over the plain and through the valleys of the shadow of death. And God caught hold of the foot of the wolf who stealthily trod and held it fast, and propped open the mouth of the bear so that he could not bite and a slavering chain hung down from his hapless jaws, silver in the moonlight. The man strode on, sleeping.

The moon called softly, "O Maker of the World, shall I stay my course so that I may light his way when he returns?" (for she had stood still, so, for Joshua thousands of years past).

But God answered, "He does not need your light. He sleeps. I will move all calamities and distresses from his path. I am his keeper. Go on your way." So obediently she continued to traverse the sky.

The man strode on even into the desert. And an eagle-owl in a dead date-palm tree, he who is large as a man, whose huge wings spread like a sailing ship blocked out the drifting moon, screamed harshly, "Who is this man who strides so boldly through the night as if it is his not mine," and would have swooped upon him. But God curled his talons so tightly round the branch, he could not loosen them.

The man did not cease his stride until he came to a mountain, and in the side of the mountain was a cave, the Cave of Machpelah. In this cave lay the Three Gifts, and here lay all who had once held them.

Here lay Adam, and Eve of the coyly braided hair (but not Lilith the equal, for the Gifts belonged to the time when she had proudly left the Garden). And here lay Seth who had built the pillars of mysteries, and Methuselah who slew demons, and Noah of the first rainbow, and Nimrod of the seven thrones, and Abraham who had marvelled at the Tower of Babel, with his wife Sarah, one of the four most beautiful women in the world; and here lay Rebekah, and Isaac who at sight of her at last gave up mourning for Sarah his mother; and here lay Jacob the schemer, side by side with Leah (for Rachel his dearly-beloved lay, mourned, on the road to Bethlehem). Many more waited there, waited with the Cloak, and the Staff, and the Book.

The man, still sleeping, put a hand from the darkness of the night into the deeper darkness of the cave, and took up the Gifts one by one. Still sleeping, still unseeing, he turned, and carried them home past the staring eyes of the creatures of the night. He set them down, and lay on his bed again, still sleeping. He did not wake till morning. Then for the first time he saw them. He marvelled. And he rose, and hid them.

The name of this man was Adam. (For since the time of the first man-and-woman-in-one, many have borne that name). All his life he had pondered over secrets and mysteries. He had read and he had thought and read again. And still he shook his head, and said, "There is more to know. I must know it." And in his sleep he had gone forth and claimed the Cloak, the Book and the sapphire Staff.

Now Adam had a son. They had great love for each other, and tenderly talked, and held each other, and read many books together till candle after candle flickered, and burned down. And always Adam thought of the day when his son would be ready for Adam to show him the Book of Mysteries that he had brought back from the cave in a dream. "We will read that also," he thought, "just as Jacob once read it with Joseph." For he knew the words of the Book must be passed on, as must the Cloak and the Staff.

But as day followed day, and year followed year, he saw that the boy, though learned and full of grace, and loving and so beloved, no longer pursued the answers to silent questions as he had once done, saying, "There is more to be known," but was now content with what he already knew. And Adam thought sorrowfully, "He is not the one"; and he did not show him the Book.

So did many years pass. And the man called Adam grew old. Now he puckered his brow with the effort of seeing, and his back grew more and more bent like one who curves himself round his heart as one curves a hand round a flickering candleflame. And he said to himself incessantly, "Who is it who shall have the Gifts after me?" For he knew he was not allowed to die till he found the one who should have them.

Then one night he dreamed a dream. And in his dream a voice said, "There is a boy in the city of Okopy who is now grown. His name is Israel, son of Eliezer. The Book, the Cloak and the Staff are his."

Adam awoke. He washed. He dressed with great care. He called to his child and held him to him, and he said, "My son, we have studied many books together, you and I. But there is one I have not shown you."

And his son said, "Was I not worthy of it?"

And Adam said, "It is not your destiny. It would burn you with its fire. It is for another."

And he told him what had been said in the dream. "It is for one named Israel, son of Eliezer, in the city of Okopy. You must find him, and give him the Book, together with the Cloak and the sapphire Staff. Do not be sad. It is a great honour for you. You are the squire who gives the sword to his knight and master, the sword that was tempered by those now lying silent." And he took the Book, the Cloak, and the Staff from their hiding place, and gave them to him.

Then at last Adam could die, for he was very old, and had lived so long only because he was waiting. And his son buried him with honour. And the son went forth to find the boy.

The Captive and his Wife

And now it was as if a sparrow had tentatively called from a rooftop, when the moon had become a pale ghost, and it was still not light. And a song and a story began again, like another bird calling, and here is it told.

For when Adam asked God, "To whom must I give the Three Gifts?" and waited for his dream, a certain far-off village was captured by bandits. And among those captured was a man named Eliezer.

Eliezer had a wife. But her name is nowhere told, for these were still the days after Lilith, when women were no longer much spoken of by name. But she was known among other women for wisdom and skill. And though the Book of All Knowledge Worth Knowing was now hid from humankind, some of its pages were already writ unseen in her mind.

She slipped out of the bandits' hands, and twisting here and there, for she knew the paths well, she escaped into the mountains. And here women sought her when the time of birth was upon them. And always she said to them with sureness, "Eliezer will return."

But while she had fled away, the bandits had dragged the rest of the villagers into boats, and chained them to the oars. And they had made them row to a far-off country. And there they had pulled the boats up on the shore.

And men came to stare at the captives, and fingered them and looked in their mouths as if they were cattle, and took out gold and bought them for slaves. So had it happened to Joseph, thousands of years before, Joseph of the lustrous coat and the dreams. And so it happened to Eliezer, that he was bought.

And as with Joseph, Eliezer served the master who bought him faithfully and well, so well that his master made him steward of his whole house.

Joseph had wanted power. But Eliezer only secretly longed for his wife, for he loved her as his own soul, and his heart ached that he was in a strange land, where the air blew differently and with a different touch.

Each night as he lay down to sleep he made intricate plans for escape. But each night, as his eyes closed, a dream said to him, "Wait. The time is not yet come." And he awoke to the same wind that blew differently, the wind of a foreign land, and when he turned on his side there was no-one there.

Now it came to pass that one day his master wished to ask some large favour of the viceroy of the King, and had need of a gift to give him. So he gave to him Eliezer, saying, "Take him. He is my gift to you. He is full of grace and wisdom, and he has been my right hand. Let him be yours." And the King's viceroy took Eliezer as gift, as one might take an ox or a swift horse.

But he saw Eliezer was truly a gift of greatness, that he was a man to be loved. So that he did not ask for work, but gave him, in respect, a room to study in. All that he asked in return was that when he returned home, Eliezer would wash his feet; for this was the custom. So they lived together in harmony. And at night Eliezer wove his own plans, dreamed, and still waited. For so the dream told him.

Now it came to pass that the King engaged in war with his enemies, and he sent his army to enter their city. But the city was strong and well-guarded, and they could not enter it.

So sent the King for his viceroy, that was the master of Eliezer. And the King said to him, "My army is ready to lay waste the enemy, and waits impatient outside the city, the horses pawing the ground. But they cannot find a way in. Have you counsel for me?" But the viceroy was not a man of war, and he had no counsel to offer, and the King was filled with anger against him and sent him away.

So the viceroy returned home, and Eliezer would have welcomed him home, and bathed his feet as he always did. But the viceroy would have none of it, and would not be touched, but lay on a couch, brooding with hidden eyes.

And Eliezer said, "Why are you troubled, master?" and receiving no answer asked him again and again, gently insisting, even to endangering himself.

Till at last the viceroy said, "The King needs to enter the city of his enemy, and I could not advise him. So is he wroth with me, and I with myself."

Then Eliezer said, "I will ask my God a dream-question. He understands war, as he understands peace. And she is a revealer of secrets, and will send me a dream-answer."

And in the night, Eliezer asked the dream-question. And God answered the question, and explained all the secrets of the battle to him.

And some songs say his dream showed him iron pillars planted in the water, to overturn boats that sought the city; and how a hidden pathway wove between, for those who knew to tread in it. And others say the dream showed him a great stone by the water's edge; and when the stone rolled away, there was a hole, and the hole was the mouth of a tunnel, and the tunnel led into the city, and the leader had but to take a candle, and the soldiers would follow. The dream-answer is different in different stories, but all say the question was answered.

Then said the King to the viceroy, "Are you a sorcerer? Whence had you these secrets?"

And the viceroy said, "It was not I, but my slave, Eliezer, who knew."

Then did the King say, "Send him to me!" And he heaped honours upon Eliezer and made him Commander of Battles, so that he became known to all in the land, and songs were sung of him. And all that he undertook prospered.

But still as night came by and Eliezer lay down, the old thoughts beat in his head like ceaseless drums, and he cried out aloud, "If I were with my wife again!" But the dream said, "Wait. The time has not yet come."

So years went by. And it came to pass that the viceroy died. And the King gave the daughter of the viceroy to Eliezer to be his wife (for this was long after Lilith who was proud and free, and it was the custom). But Eliezer's thoughts were of his own wife, who had escaped from the bandits years before. He did not know if she were alive or dead, but he longed for her. So he did not touch the viceroy's daughter, nor did he speak to her too much, nor go too close.

And at last she said to him, "Why do you not touch me? What fault do you find in me?"

And now a voice said to him, "This is the time. Speak!"

And Eliezer said, "I find no fault in you. You are gracious to me beyond words. But I have a wife already, and I long for her." And he told her how he had been captured years before and taken to this land that was strange to him, and how his wife had escaped and was he knew not where, and how every night he longed for her.

And the viceroy's daughter saw that his soul was knit with the soul of his wife, and she paid him great honour. "You shall be where you wish to be," she said. And she commanded for him a ship to sail in, and sailors to row with many oars. And she ordered the ship to be filled with silver and gold and precious silk, and woods that made his head faint with their sweet smell. And she sent him back over the sea to Okapi, where he longed to be.

And it is said in song and story that bandits followed him over the sea, hunting him down for the treasure that he carried, and he cried out to them, "Take it! Take all I own. What is gold and silver? All I long for is my wife and the land where she waits for me! Take everything, and do not delay me!" And astounded, they took the treasure, and the ship sped on.

And at that moment God looked out over all the devastated world, and said, "The Gifts are ready."

And God saw Eliezer alone on the sea, longing, and Eliezer's wife in the mountains, waiting. And God put out a hand, one to each, and drew them together. And although each was now a hundred years old, so long had been the waiting, they had a child. And like the stirrings of birds in the morning, one answering another, songs and stories began again.

THE CHARCOAL BURNER

Eliezer and his wife, being more than a hundred years old, lay down and died. For when the world was new and empty, time and space were different, and there was no nearness or farness, or early and late, and men and women spread out into many years. But now a hundred years was enough.

Whether the child's mother whispered to him when she was dying is nowhere recorded. For after Lilith the tousled-haired, even the songs tried not to hear women's voices. But the last words of his father are still told in song and story. And he said, "Though the earth do change, and the mountains be moved into the heart of the sea, never fear. For you will carry my candle, and it will light up the world."

The people of the village took care of the child. They fed him. They clothed him. They sent him to school. But the child would not stay there. Each day he ran away.

The schoolteacher would search for him, and would find him in the woods, and take his hand and lead him back. But as soon as he let go the child's hand, again he would slip away, back to the river that glinted, back to the trees that rustled, the little beasts that scurried secretly in the undergrowth. For how can the net hold fast the sea?

And he would lie all day in the grass, looking up through the leaves at the glowing sky, and listening to the to-and-fro of the talk of the birds. And he was so silently joyful that at last the teacher shrugged his shoulders and said, "He is a simpleton. He is not fit for learning, not a wise one like his father." And he left him to do as he pleased.

And the child ate with the birds and the woodland creatures, and he joined his voice with theirs. And thousands of years after the Garden of Delight, the child heard one voice that united the silence and made it vibrate like a bell.

When he was ten years old and ready to work, the child came back to the village. His work was to go from one house to another, wakening the children and leading them to school, and in the evening bringing them back again. And when he had done this for a very little while, the people said, "Something is stirring in our children. They are changing."

For they sang, these children, they sang in their long line as they followed their shepherd, first he singing, then one by one all singing.

He would gather them in the early morning, then he would lead them away from the schoolhouse, and round in a huge circle, through the fields and through the woods, till they came back to the schoolhouse again. And they would be carrying green branches in their hands, with flowers woven in their hair, and on the flowers butterflies slowly opening and closing their wings as they went, and the birds dipping and skimming and circling their heads, and the children singing. And in this way they would enter the schoolhouse.

And it is said in song and story that their singing spiralled up to heaven like the song of a skylark, and it trickled like a meandering stream all over the earth, soaking into the parched soil. And God heard the song in heaven, and Sammael, leader of the fallen angels, whom some called Lucifer, Son of the Dawn, or Iblis or Satan or Azazel (for he is known in many places and by many names), heard it also. And Sammael was filled with rage at the joy in the song of human beings, for he had plotted against them from the beginning of time. And he shouted to God, "I will destroy them!"

And God said, "They are only children."

But Sammael demanded, "Let me strive against them!"

And God nodded, saying, "Strive."

Then Sammael became small as a crumb, as he had become thousands of years before when he had hidden under the snake's tongue to persuade Eve. And he crept under stones where beetles scurried, dull ones and shining ones, and up the stalks of flowers where clung green insects, and into the honeyed heart of the flower itself, jostling the bees that foraged there and silkily asking their pardon, and into the crevices of the bark of trees where creeping things hurried and birds dug with their pointed beaks; and he said to everything that lived, "Dear living things, I have poison. Take it for me to this child, that he will die."

But they would not do so. And Sammael crackled and spluttered like a live coal, and became large again, and cast about what he should do.

It was then he remembered the charcoal-burner.

In the wood, the wood where the child had lived, lived an old charcoal-burner who did not know good from bad, nor his right hand from his left. His body lived and ate and slept; but he had been born without a human soul; and he hid himself in the forest for he was ashamed. And because he hid himself, the people feared him; and because they feared him, he was afraid also.

And some said he was a sorcerer. And they were not wholly wrong. For at night a sick power took possession of the old charcoal-burner. And his hands and his feet turned into shaggy paws, and he walked on them, howling. And the villagers said to their children, "Do not go late into the woods. A werewolf lives there."

Yet he had never hurt anyone, for he was ashamed of his sickness. And though he prowled in the wood and howled when the fit was on him (for he could not help himself), as soon as it grew weaker, he would creep into bushes and lie there panting till he fell asleep.

And there asleep in a bush, Sammael found him. Sammael put out his hand, and took out the old charcoal-burner's heart, which was innocent as a child, and buried it in the earth; and in its place he put his own heart, that had been plotting, in anguish, since the very beginning of time.

In the morning, the charcoal-burner awoke. And when the boy led the singing children into the woods, he leapt from the bushes and rushed at them with eyes red as the winter sun, and teeth like jagged birch trees struck by lightning. The children screamed, and some fell down insensible, and some fled this way and that in panic, and some clung to each other and sobbed. But the werewolf had disappeared.

Then the village people hastened to seek their children, those who had not fled home weeping with terror, and they said, "It is that boy Israel" (for that was his name). "He does not respect boundaries. They shall not go with him again."

But the boy heard again in his heart his father saying, "Never fear." And he walked into the wood.

All day he walked there, alone, listening to the voices of the wood. Then he returned to the village, and he went from house to house, saying to the fathers and mothers, "Let the children come with me. It was only a wolf who ran by them. He was frightened of the children. Let them come again with me tomorrow."

And they looked into his eyes which were earnest and

calm and steady, and they trusted him, and said, "Tomorrow."

So the next morning, the boy Israel gathered again all the children of the village, and he spoke to them of love and of joy and of the power of song, and he calmed them. And he set off singing, and the children followed him, also singing... in a circle, across the fields, and up to the edge of the forest. And he said to them, "Remain here." And he went into the forest alone.

And the werewolf with the heart of Sammael saw him coming, and came forth to meet him. And as he came, his shaggy paws grew as large as flat-topped mountains and clutched the four corners of the earth, and his back rose up into a dome that fitted into the curve of the sky, and his eyes were like throbbing furnaces. But the boy walked forward.

He came up to the werewolf. He walked forward between the shaggy paws of the werewolf. He walked forward into the cloud of hot breath of the werewolf. He walked into the very body of the werewolf. And he walked up to the very heart of the werewolf as it beat inside him, the heart that was Sammael's, glowing with the hatred of thousands of years. And the boy put out his hand and closed it over the heart and held it tight. And he felt its trembling, and he felt its shuddering, and he felt its fear and the pain and anguish of thousands of years, and its crying. And he was filled with pity for the hating heart, and he set it free on the earth. And the earth opened, and swallowed it.

In the evening, the villagers found the old charcoal-burner lying dead in the forest, smiling like a child. And they said to each other, "Why were we ever afraid of him? He was just a child."

THE SWEEPER

Now it is said in song and story that after the battle for the heart of Sammael, the thirst for more knowledge burned in the boy Israel. And he said, "I must know more. There must be more to know." And he left the village where the children sang, and returned to the little town of Okapi where he was born.

And there he found the house of study where people came to pray. And he became a sweeper there. He swept up spiders and shadows, and shuffled his feet in the corners. And the only sound he made was sneezing in the dust, being almost a shadow himself.

And the people, if they ever saw him - for he was not someone to be seen and noticed - only smiled and shook their heads in pity. But when they went home at night, he took books from the shelves, lit a candle, and read, and read, and read more, never stopping till the first cock-crow splintered the darkness.

And now Ben Adam, which means the son of Adam, had taken the Cloak and the Book and the sapphire Staff, and left the city of his birth. And he was searching for the boy.

He asked as he went, "Do you know Israel, son of Eliezer, a learned boy?" But all shook their heads, for they did not. In village after village, he asked; but none could tell him of a learned boy.

At last he came to the town of Okapi. The people of Okapi received him with honour, for they remembered his father Adam, and spoke of him with love. But they knew of no-one learned, named Israel son of Eliezer. And he was perplexed, for his destiny was to find him.

One evening he stayed in the house of study after everyone else had left. Only the boy remained, sweeping the floor. He looked at the face of the sweeper, and it was strangely calm, the face of one that hears a silent song.

The next day he said to the elders, "Give me the boy for my servant. I need to study. I shall read far into the night."

"Why do you ask for him?" they said. "Choose a child more able. This one is nothing but a senseless clod. He does not even open his mouth. All he can do is sweep the dust." Yet even so, a memory stirred in them. And they said among themselves "His father was Eliezer." And they sighed and said, "Who would have thought the son of a wise man would be such a simpleton!" And "It must be to honour Eliezer, and in pity and kindness for the boy, that Ben Adam has chosen him."

When the boy came to him, Ben Adam said, "What is your name?"

And he said, "I am Israel, son of Eliezer."

That night Ben Adam lay down on the bench, and he pretended to sleep. And through the fringe of his eyelashes he saw the boy Israel quietly take a candle, and light it, and stand with a book in his hands. And the son of Adam, watching him through the narrow cracks of his eyes, was reminded of his own father, for he too had read in the same way, standing motionless for hours while the candle burned, as if the words had cast a spell on him and invisible hands held him.

In the morning, the growing light overtook the candleflame, the boy sighed, his body folded up in weariness, and he slept.

Then Ben Adam, who had watched him all night long, arose and he took one separate page from the Book of All Knowledge Worth Knowing and placed it on the boy's breast, and it rose and fell with his breathing, and fluttered now and then in the air he breathed out.

The boy stretched out a hand in his sleep, as if he heard the fluttering, and took hold of the paper. He carried it up to his eyes. Then he opened his eyes. Then he read. Then he rose up. And his whole face was ablaze. And he read the whole page from start to finish. And at the end he swayed, and fell on the bench again, and slept.

Ben Adam came and sat beside him. And when he thought he was near waking again, he put out his hand and took the boy's hand, the hand that still held one page of the Book of All Knowledge, and he opened the boy's fingers and put in that hand all the rest of the Book. And he said to the boy's closed eyes, "Hear me. When no-one on earth was worthy of it, it was hidden from humankind. It was found again. It was lost again. It was once more found. My father held it, with the Cloak and the Sword. But it was not my destiny to hold it after him. My destiny was to find you, and give it in your keeping, and to serve you." And the boy opened his eyes, and the two looked into each other's faces.

And the boy said, "Do not speak to anyone yet of my power. The time has not come."

And the boy rose up, and said, "We need no rule books, but only the open sky. We need no buildings, but only the forest. We need no prohibitions, but only joy in every living thing." And they went out together, out of the building and out of the city, till the time should be come.

THE ANGER OF THE LAKE

The boy waited, till at last he dreamed a dream. And the dream said, "Now! The time has come! Unite the splintered world!"

And many many songs began to be sung, till the air was full again of words and notes of music, and it was like the joyous bustle of an early morning; and the words of storytellers once again drew people after them as a flock follows the shepherd, piping.

And every day was a celebration. And one would turn cartwheels, and one would whistle, and one would leap backwards and forwards over the brook, and one would whirl round and around. And the wise men who prayed only in buildings said, "They are mad!" for they could not hear the music to which they danced. And those who loved him called Israel 'Master of the Good Name'.

And it is said in song and story that in his universe none were left out, and the water-carrier and the mule-driver sat at his long table and ate and danced and sang with learned men.

And whoever needed him he came to, travelling from one end of the earth to the other in a single night, for there were no boundaries of time or place for him. His little horse would trot along the lane, then the jolting of his cart would become a skimming and a sailing and a flying, and the air would smell of a sudden strangely sweet, and the stars in the sky would laugh as the little horse weaved among them.

Now it is told in song and story that Israel had a cousin, a careless man, whose name was Schmerl. All year long he committed evil carelessly, and bundled it out of the way into his basement. And each New Year's Eve he pulled the bundles out, and dragged them down to the lake's edge, and kicked them and pummelled them and pushed them till they fell in.

"One or two more, what does it matter," said Schmerl, laughing. "But it is lucky the lake is so near. It would be a nuisance to carry them further."

Year by year the water grew blacker and more and more angry. And one year Schmerl committed such a huge ugly evil that he could scarcely find a place to store it till the New Year came. He dragged it down to the basement, but it dripped and it oozed, and the smell of it came up through the floorboards and made strange white patches on the wood, and grey clouds formed, like old spiders' webs, and clung to it.

On New Year's Day, Schmerl took hold, and sometimes dragging, sometimes pulling, he heaved it down to the lake, little by little, and breathlessly kicked it in.

The lake grew blacker still with rage. It boiled. It heaved. It reared itself up. But it could not get rid of the huge stinking evil. It swirled into whirlpools, and frothed with anger. But it could not get rid of it. And it remembered that at the very beginning of time the waters were doomed to receive the evils of humankind, and there was nothing the lake could do to escape its destiny. Therefore it grew calm, and began to work hard to cleanse itself. But it vowed revenge.

Now Schmerl and his wife were growing old, yet still they had no children. And his wife said, "We have no children because of the evil that you throw into the water year after year, continuously."

But Schmerl said, "I will go to my cousin, Israel, whom people call Master of the Good Name. If he can do miracles for strangers, let him do one for his own family."

So he talked with Israel. And Israel shook his head when he looked at him; and as Schmerl talked and laughed and shrugged his shoulders, he shook his head again. But he remembered Schmerl's wife, who was loving and whole-hearted, and he said at last, "Go home. I can promise you only that you will have a son."

"Only?" said Schmerl, astonished. "But that is what I asked!"

Months passed, and Schmerl's wife gave birth to a beautiful boy. She sent Schmerl to Israel, to thank him. But when Schmerl entered the cottage, the Master looked up at him, with his eyes full of sorrow, and he said, "On his thirteenth birthday, your son will die in the lake."

Schmerl threw himself down on the floor and cried out, "No!"

And Israel said, "You have made the lake angry. Every year you threw evil into it, more each year; and that last terrible oozing stinking evil was more than it would bear."

But Schmerl cried out again, "Help me!"

And the Master said, "There is one chance. On his thirteenth birthday, keep the child away from the water."

"Of course!" said Schmerl. "I will do it." And he smiled.

"It is not so easy," said Israel. "Do you think you will remember in thirteen years?"

And Schmerl smiled again. "Of course."

Israel sighed. "Listen to me. On the day of your son's thirteenth birthday, when you begin to dress yourself, you will put your two stockings on your left foot. That is a sign, and you must remember." And because he saw Schmerl was not listening seriously, he held him by the coat, and said, "Tell your wife! Tell all your household also! Tell them also that on the day you cannot find your second stocking a terrible thing will happen!"

But Schmerl thought, "Why should I tell anyone? I will remember." And he returned home, and told no-one. And he forgot.

Now the boy who was born was beautiful. And he grew strong and swift, and swam and leaped like a curving dolphin in the water, and all smiled to see him.

On the morning of the boy's thirteenth birthday, Schmerl woke, and did not remember. He began to dress, and his head ached with the heat of the sun. He put on one stocking. He stopped to wipe the sweat from his face. Without thinking or looking, he drew the other stocking on to the same foot. He looked for the stocking for his right foot which was bare. He emptied cupboards. He looked under chairs. He pulled drawers open and slammed them shut, and shouted with rage, and with the overwhelming heat of the morning.

"What is it?" his wife said, waking.

"It is my other stocking," he shouted at her. "It vanished! I had it in my hand, and then it vanished."

She looked at him, stared at his leg, and began to laugh. "But there it is, Schmerl," she said. "They are both on one leg!"

He remembered. He ran to the room where his son slept. The boy was not there. He ran to the doorway of the house, and he saw, already a distance off, his son on the way to the lake. "Come back!" he shouted, "Come back!"

But the boy looked over his shoulder and called back,

"It is hot. I want to swim."

"Come back!" cried Schmerl, but the boy ran on.

So with one leg covered and one leg bare, Schmerl ran after his son. The boy was swift and ran with ease. "Master of the Good Name, help me again!" cried Schmerl. And at that moment the boy tripped over the root of a tree.

Before he could get to his feet, his father was at his side, and had gripped his arm. He dragged the boy home and locked him in his room.

The boy hammered on the door. "Let me out!" he shouted. But his father would not open it. The boy screamed, "It is hot! I can scarcely breathe! Let me out! Let me go to the lake!" But his father would not open the door.

"Why do you imprison me! What have I done! What crime have I committed! Give me at least a dish of water to bathe my face! It is too hot to bear!" But he would not give him even that, for he was afraid of the water.

At noonday the sun was high in the sky, blazing down on the water. The lake was filled with swimmers. The water began to heave. Then it began to swirl. Then in the middle of the swirling and the whirling and the foaming, an arm broke the surface, and it reached up into the air. Then a second arm broke the surface. And it too reached into the air. Then a head broke the surface, a monstrous ugly head. And all were wreathed and tangled and dripping with seaweed. And the blazing angry eyes of the head stared round into all the faces one by one. And the mouth opened. "The Hour has come, but One is missing!" shouted the mouth. And it howled, a long, long howl.

Then the head and the arms sank back into the water, and the white waves of the foaming lake dissolved till there were only little flecks of cream, and long torn strands of seaweed that floated away on the water.

The sun set. Schmerl and his wife entered the room. The boy lay exhausted on the floor of his room. Tenderly they woke him, and they gave him sweet wine to drink, and almonds and raisins and little pancakes, for was it not the feast of his birthday?

And Schmerl threw no more evil into the water.

THE DANCE

One day many people were waiting for Israel. Each had a question to ask him, and each believed that this one question deserved an immediate answer.

He entered the room. He saw their urgent faces. He heard their eager breathing. He felt their unspoken questions darting this way and that like dragonflies in the air.

But he did not ask them to voice their questions. Instead, very very softly he began to hum.

"Hmm. Hmm." Sweetly and tunefully.

Some were merely surprised. Some were offended. Some were angry.

But after a while, someone else in the room began to hum also, shyly, sweetly, picking up the tune with him. And then another. And another. And in a little while, everyone in the room was humming together, softly and gently.

Then in the same gentle way, Israel began to sing, putting words to the melody. And after a while another joined in, shyly; and then another. Till one by one all in the room were adding the words, and all were singing.

And then Israel took a step, and another step, and he began to dance to the singing. And one by one, at first shyly, then with confidence, then with amazement at themselves, then with abandonment, all in the room were dancing – more and more joyfully, more and more wildly, with more and more laughter, till the stars in the sky outside picked up the rhythm, and danced and laughed with them. But although they danced with abandon, yet were they aware of each other, so that the whole room was a pattern of moving bodies that gracefully gave way without pausing and without ceasing their flow, so that each was both separate and together like a flock of birds in the sky.

For a long time they danced. Then gradually Israel began to slow his dancing, and he began to quiet his singing. And all began gradually to dance more gently and to sing more softly.

And at last, almost imperceptibly, his dance moved into stillness. And one by one all were still. And all was silent.

And into the silence, for the first time, he spoke. "I trust I have answered all your questions," he said. And he smiled, and left them.

The Next

The two friends stood outside the Mountain. Inside the Mountain, all who had once held the Three Gifts of God waited silently. Adam who betrayed Lilith was there, and Eve of the braided hair, Noah of the crowded Ark and of the first tender Rainbow, Jacob who schemed and loved, and Joseph who was beautiful as an olive-tree and who dreamed dreams; and there were many more, keeping watch in the dark.

Then Israel spoke the one Word, and the Mountain obediently opened.

Into the black emptiness, the same black emptiness towards which one night the father of Ben Adam, sleeping, had walked unhesitatingly, he placed the Three Gifts of God. The Staff that is blue as the sapphire sky, with its one powerful Name, All-That-Is. The Cloak that smells of the fields of Delight and has pictured on it every animal, every bird, every fish in the universe, and once lifted Solomon on the wings of the wind. And the Book of All Knowledge, in which are signs of calamity, and blessing also, and the Song of the Sun and the Thoughts of the Rain and the Language of all Creation.

He also did not hesitate. He placed them in the black emptiness with trust. And it was as if he placed them into a huge hand that was waiting in the dark and the hand held them, for his friend Ben Adam, listening, did not hear them fall.

"The earth is crying," said Israel. "So may the Next come soon, whoever the Next may be. Then shall the sad trees leap for joy. And Man and Woman again be one. The Wolf once more shall lie with the Lamb, and none learn war any more."

Then suddenly, unexpectedly, he threw back his head and roared with laughter. "Who would ever have thought the Next would once have been Jacob!" He shook his head from side to side, wiping his eyes. "Jacob, that scoundrel!" And his friend looked at him, and laughed also. And the sound of them both echoed and bounced round the Mountain like a loose rock falling.

Quietened, he spoke the Word again, and the mountain closed. And the moss ran swiftly again over the cracks like trickling water and sealed it as if it had never been opened.

Then Israel and Ben Adam stepped slowly away, two old men side by side, as Moses and Aaron had once stepped side by side among the fawning lions of Pharaoh.

And inside the darkness of the Mountain, the snakeskin Cloak and the sapphire Staff and the Book of All Knowledge that is Worth to be Known, glowed, as they had done long ago in the night-times of the Ark, calmly alert to re-enter time.

That is the song and the story.

ACKNOWLEDGEMENTS

I am indebted to the following:

The many volumes of *Legends of the Jews* by Louis Ginzberg; *Hebrew Myths* by Robert Graves and Raphael Patai; *Myth, Legend and Custom in the Old Testament* by Theodore Gaster (including chapters from *Folklore in the Old Testament* by Sir James Frazer); *Myth and Legend of Ancient Israel* by A.S. Rappoport; *Antiquities of the Jews by Josephus; Folk Lore of the Holy Land* by J.E. Hanauer; *Bible History of the Old Testament* by A. Edersheim; *Literary Guide to the Bible* edited by R. Alter and F. Kermode; *Hebrew and Babylonian Traditions* by N. Jastrow; *Irony in the Old Testament* by Edwin Good; *The Jewish Encyclopaedia; The Hebrew Scriptures* by S. Sandmel; *The Golden Mountain* by M. Levin; *In Praise of the Baal Shem Tov* translated and edited by D. Ben-Amos and J.R. Mintz; *Legends of Jerusalem* by Zev Vilnay; various collections such as *A Treasury of Jewish Folklore* edited by N. Ausbel, *Treasures of the Talmud* edited by S. Levy, *Tales from the Talmud* by E.R. Montague, *The Talmud* translated by H. Polano; and *Jacob Makes It Across the Jabbok* by Heather McKay in *The Journal for the Study of the Old Testament*. The editions of the Old Testament I used were *The Bible Designed to be Read as Literature* (by Ernest Sutherland Bates with introduction by Laurence Binyon), which has delighted me since the thirties, and the volumes of the Soncino Bible in Hebrew and English, which belonged to my mother.

My thanks also to the Leo Baeck Library in the Sternberg Centre, London, and to the St. Deiniol Residential Library in Hawarden, Clywd, North Wales, whose joint resources I found invaluable when I started on this book in 1986.